The

TRANSFORMATION
Promise

A book about love, healing and the flow of life

with love & light,

[signature]

Johanna Derbolowsky

To find out more about Johanna, or to book her
for your next event, visit her website
quantumheartfield.com
or email her directly at jd@quantumheartfield.com

Ready to journey to a better life experience?
for 25% off any workshop or 1 hour private
session use code: thesource18
New clients only. Expires 11/20/20

QUANTUM
HEART FIELD ©2011

D1400506

Author's Note

Please note that all names and stories from clients are changed to ensure confidentiality and privacy. Even though the events are true the settings, names and circumstances are changed beyond personal recognition.

The Transformation Promise

ISBN 978-1495359347
2nd edition January 2014
Cover design by Eva Machauf
Copyright 2012 © All rights reserved.
http://TheTransformationPromise.com

No part of this work may be reproduced or transmitted in any form or by any means, electronic or mechanical, including photocopying and recording, or by any information storage or retrieval system, without prior permission in written form from the publisher.

For my amazing children Max and Sophie

Contents

Acknowledgements

My favorite part of writing and publishing this book is saying thanks to all the people who held my hand and those who pushed me from the safety of what I knew and made me seek my own expansion. Some of you passed through my life quickly and others stayed for the long run. Whether it was kind support or a painful encounter that pushed me to excel past my self-imposed limits, I am grateful. There are many of you and I can't mention all of you, but if you are and were ever in my life: I thank you for your support.

I would especially like to thank my parents for giving me a way into this world and for having been just who they were, so I could become who I am; and in the same breath I want to thank my siblings, Sonja, Jakob, Karina, my sister in-law Renate, my step mother Regina and brother Markus; and special thanks to Luise Abeldt, my nanny, I can't imagine my life without you. I want to thank my children Max and Sophie for always being there to show me without mercy when I am off track and to support me when I am back on track. You are the best! Michael Albert for supporting me even if it made no sense to you, you taught me a lot.

A special thanks to my teachers, the ones who didn't inspire me directly for showing me how not to teach and the ones that inspired me for lighting flames deep within myself to seek and move on. I had so many great teachers that I can't mention all of them, but favorites are Osvaldo Cettour and Dr. Bueb for listening to me when I was down and out without judging me, Mr Doleschall, who without ever asking questions stood by me during difficult times.

I want to thank Lotte Bonz and Friedel Mann for showing me that life gets better and better; my friend Michael Lawler who taught me to treat myself as if I were my favorite lover. James T. Russel and Robert Kobashi, my art teachers who taught me how to see beyond images and how to find the answer within; Dini Clark who taught me how to teach from the heart, I miss you. Dr. Nossrat Peseshkian who in a two hour conversation changed my life from deep depression to hopeful joy; Dr. Arthur Bassin, who showed me that I can find the positive element in everything.

My healing teachers, especially Theo Schlegel, who inspired my curiosity for homeopathy and healing; Bruder Innozenz, who taught me many essentials of healing; my grandmother for showing me infinity and the other side; the Zen master who taught me to think and move with spirit leading the body, thank you.

I thank all the magical people who helped me write this book, encouraged me to do better than I thought I could, without you there would be no book; my incredible author friend Annegret Heinold, Peter Winkler, the poet Marcellus, Betsy Gael, Sue Sutton, Uschi And Ecki Buchberger and my phenomenal editor Molly Kochan you are pure magic.

I also want to name some of my friends who inspired parts of the book, and I have the best friends, Gunter Benz, Manfred Gans, Julia Johnsen, Elisabeth Siegmann, Julia Nelson, Richard Marriott, Bernadette Schlee, Michael and Gretchen Moore, Deanna Jordan, Clare Pilates, Jessica Taylor, Larry Washington, Dr. Thomas and Dr. Claudia Mueller, who opened their home and family to me and held the writing and teaching space for me; and Ben Vereen, who pushed me further and faster on my path than anyone; I especially want to thank Denise Dean, Janis Taylor and Eva Machauf, who put up with all my growth periods, joys and fears and stand by me with their support holding me up when I am falling down, shining their light on me so I can always be in a bright space, I feel like the luckiest person on earth, thank you!

Introduction

Everything starts out with a thought, a feeling, a dream. Dreaming is an essential tool in life. In our dreams we can play out scenarios, come up with solutions or find new directions. Once we have a dream and we get excited about it we put energy into it. It is like adding fuel to a car, and then all that is left is starting the car and driving toward our dream and goal. But if it is that easy, then why do dreams not always work out? This is a common question I get from my students, clients and one question I have asked myself over and over again. There are two reasons for this.

One is that we think we have a dream, when instead our dream is something that society has made us believe we want. No matter how perfectly we concentrate and visualize on the achievement of this dream and work towards it, it may elude us. Because there is always the overriding soul purpose and growth that will guide us in the direction we need to go for our true dream.

The other reason is because we get into our dream car and we forget to look where we are going. We look over our shoulder at our starting point rather than to where we are going. At the same time we leave our foot on the gas and inevitably we crash, believing that our goal, dream or direction wasn't the right one for us, when instead the problem was in our not keeping our eye on the road ahead. After the crash comes the healing of wounds, repairing the old car, or getting a new one and starting out again and again. Our inner GPS still knows the direction we want to go in and will let us know where that is and where we are in relation to it. So we set out, often times crashing before we ever get restarted. This is a cycle that is often repeated before any change happens. The purpose of this book is to show you how to look ahead and how to connect to that inner GPS so you continue to move in the direction of your dreams.

Sometimes your GPS may reroute because of unforeseen circumstances so the other purpose of this book is to encourage you to "go with the flow." If you can learn to navigate your journey with ease, chances are your destinations will turn out better than you could have dreamed. The Universe will always supply us with what we need. Sometimes this is the same as what we want at the moment and sometimes it is not, until long after that we realize, we got exactly what we really wanted and needed.

Growing up I met and learned from different healers and shaman. Deep down inside I had a strong wish to become like them. There was just one problem: all of them were Zen masters, monks, or otherwise reclusive people and I was a girl of the world. I wanted to hang out with friends, was always in love with some boy and certain that I didn't want to become a nun. For a few months I went to church regularly because I had a crush on one of the boys who attended. But most of the sermons made me feel bad. I didn't understand why God would give me the desire to enjoy life and at the same time tell me it was bad to enjoy anything. This question was present as far back as I can remember. I used to talk with my grandmother about it. She visited us a couple of times a year and we took long walks. She told me about how anyone can talk to God and get all the answers needed if one gets quiet enough to hear them. And since I was convinced that this world was seriously flawed, she told me to take my issues up with God. I tried and tried. Even though I often felt discouraged and frustrated because God seemed silent I never lost my faith. I always had just enough evidence of miracles in and around my life to know that there was more than I could understand at the moment.

Still I have crashed many times, dusted off my clothes, put on band-aids and moved on to the next adventure of life. Especially when growing up I couldn't envision how I could be worthy of gifts from the Universe. But the Universe presented me with teachers and experiences that rekindled my dream or my remembrance of why I came here. Even though I had given up on my dreams my GPS still knew the direction, and led me back to the topic of healing, to my gifts and to the desire to understand the Universe.

After I finished school in Germany I moved to Maine, New York City and later Los Angeles. I worked in the film business as a camera assistant and studied fine arts. I tried different professions and to fit myself into a "normal" life, but something always happened to shift my focus back to the desire to help and the wish to understand the Universe.

Growing up I helped in my dad's medical office. He believed that I had a gift for healing. It scared me. On the outside I moved away from all healing ideas but deep inside they grew. I couldn't lead an unconscious, superficial life and not feel depressed and empty. I tried to numb myself but it didn't work. When one of my then 4 year old relatives got sick with leukemia I was drawn to find out about Attitudinal Healing, to help deal with the situation. I signed myself up and completed the training. Intrigued by what I learned I studied the psychology of children faced with life threatening illnesses and searched for answers to healing. I read books filled with biographies of people who had healed the impossible and created miracles in their lives.

During this search I became a Hypnotherapist, Matrix Energetics Practitioner, Reiki Master, Minister, Clairvoyant Counselor, and remembered the learning I had received as a child from Shaman and Healers. I went through an extensive Clairvoyant training, then taught clairvoyant development for years. The training helped me make sense of all the energies and things I had been seeing all my life. I began to clear my own energy. I implemented all the things I learned to clear myself, forgive and let go.

When my kids were born I left the film business to be able to be a full time mom. No matter what I did the Universe always brought the subject of healing back into my life, and finally I said yes to the call instead of hiding from it. Life did not get any easier by saying "yes", but it became clearer and more focused. There were and continue to be many challenges which push me forward on my path, actually more challenges but the rewards are priceless. I welcome it all: the challenges and the rewards, the darkness and the amazing beautiful light after dawn, and most of all the incredible love all around. Life is a journey and I walk it with the desire to be the best possible me at any given moment.

What I am offering with this book is a pathway to discover the best possible you. You will see the chapters have been constructed to circle inwards, first touching on your outer layers and then revisiting those layers on deeper levels. In order to help you in the healing process, I have sprinkled reader questions or suggestions throughout. These are meant as guides, so feel free to do them all, a few or none at all. By just reading this book, you are open to the possibility of something new. And with this openness alone, you are set to gain new awareness and an enhanced life experience.

PART I

Grids, Flow And Dreams

Remember when you were a kid and you sat on small chairs, fit through the tiny doors of small houses, slept in a crib and rode small bicycles. Imagine you still had to sleep in that crib, hunch down to fit through the door to your house, and fit your knees on that old bicycle. It would be very uncomfortable if not impossible. Now imagine that there is a big house with large chairs and a comfortable bed waiting for you. It looks nice and inviting but in order to get there you have to leave the old one or, at least, what is left of it. If you stay in your kid size surroundings, your body will be forced into uncomfortable positions for long periods of time, and your sleep will not be restful or restorative, which could lead to deformities and an accelerated aging process. Life is the same way; we grow and expand constantly and our structures need to accommodate our expansion. Sometimes in order to shift we need to be kicked out of the nest to fly, and sometimes we can manage to walk out the front door. But either way, the structures around us have to change for us to expand and grow, and the best way to synchronize the inner with the outer world is to understand yourself and your structures. It is an old wisdom that even the ancient Greeks pointed out in the aphorism "Know Thyself", inscribed at the Temple of Apollo at Delphi.

If you want to build a house for yourself you first examine your needs and wants, see what fits your life, and maybe consult with experts before you start. You will design something to fit your needs in this moment. But no matter how much energy you spend designing and building your house, always remember you are not the house. The house is just the structure you live in. This is true for all the structures around us, even our own physical structure.

One of the goals of this book is to help you determine if your structures fit you or if they need to be altered. In part one we will talk about the different kinds of structures and what weaves them together. There will be general questions for you to consider or meditate on. If you are inclined, you can actively seek out the answers, otherwise, just let the questions percolate in the back of your mind, as we will revisit each structure on deeper and deeper levels in subsequent parts.

Chapter 1

Grids Of Life

Everything in the Universe, from the smallest particles to the largest bodies, is organized by a grid, a structure. Planets, stars, moons and their orbits move within a structure. If they didn't, the sun could just migrate towards us and burn everything at any moment, or move so far away that it would get too cold to live here. Everywhere you look you will find an underlying structure down to the atoms and cells in your body. Like the planets, people also orbit or move around life within a grid and structure.

For example, our social life, our way of dealing with situations, our environment, all of that is part of our structure. Life takes place within these grids and constructs, this is where we move. But we ourselves are not structure. We are the energy that flows within the grids of our lives. This means that in order to understand, heal and shift one's life, it is essential to understand the constructs that affect us and the flow that is us.

It is important to note that all structures are temporary: bodies get older, the earth shifts and moves, especially if you live in California, houses deteriorate with time etc., even our social structures change and constantly adjust to situations. This includes jobs, careers, where we live, how we live, who our friends are, our interactions with one another and how we respond to events. Much like spiders we create a temporary web of life to contain us. And while the web itself may change, what remains constant is the space within. From physics we know that most of our universe is empty space. Take a look at the nucleus of a cell or atom. The electrons, protons and neutrons move around mostly empty space. Or take the solid matter of a large container ship; if you took all of the atoms that make up that container ship and eliminate the empty space from those atoms, the matter left over could fit into a small matchbox, containing all the weight of that ship. So space is everywhere within us and all around us. This space is infinite. And it is this space that connects everything in Oneness, a space that doesn't deteriorate. In thinking about our structures, consider that we are this space, we are the life force that moves and experiences life within the grids and structures we choose.

For the purpose of explanation, I have divided structure into three different kinds: physical, mental/emotional and spiritual to help you understand and heal yourself.

When working with clients or changing my life, I have learned to look at all three aspects of structure as well as the infrastructure that connects them in order to help with any kind of permanent shifting or healing. I have studied and read many stories of instantaneous healing, have witnessed moments like that myself and experienced them in my own body. I know without a doubt that miracles are possible, I have also seen these miracles recede and regress into their prior states of being. For example a couple gets divorced only to find themselves in new relationships with the same problems as the marriage they just left.

The grass may be greener on your neighbor's lawn, but if you watered your own, yours would look the same or if you moved next door and treated their lawn the same as yours before, it will lose its vibrancy. To achieve lasting change and movement, all grids have to be involved in the shift. It is more important to change the structures of your life than it is to change symptoms or a disease. Because by changing the constructs you set the stage for healing, you open new channels for energy to flow. When you create a lasting shift in your life your conditions have to adjust.

Physical Structure

Physical structure is the function of our body. This includes our DNA, our skeletal structure, our circulatory system, everything that makes up the physical being. Through this structure we feel pain, pleasure and any kind of touch sensation. It is amazing in all the intricate ways it functions. Take a look at the body's built-in self-healing systems and processes. If you break a bone, the structure is interrupted. But by setting it back into place, the structure will self repair. If the structure remains out of place, the body will still heal to the best of its ability. What is interesting is that however the body grows back together, the healing is not done by the structure but by the energy that flows within it. Therefore if a body is dead, the bone will not heal.

Physical structure is not just our bodies, it is the world we live in. Everything around us is physical - cars, buildings, bodies, plants, stars, sun and moon. These are all physical structures we perceive as our reality. And as soon as we attach meaning and a story to a physical structure, it becomes a key element in our web of life.

Look around you and start to observe the structures that surround you. Are they useful to you?

I love the ocean, playing in it or watching it gives me pleasure, energy and inspiration. For me it is a very useful structure. Living near the ocean has always benefited me. Another useful structure is my car. It gets me to where I want to go, and of course my home, it gives me shelter and peace, but if I look inside my home there are some things whose only purpose is to be dusted off. They don't make me feel better or inspire me and whenever I notice things that just take up space, I get rid of them.

Coming back to the body, let's not forget that the body really is the most important structure, because without it we would not experience life. Be mindful of keeping this structure in shape so your essence can flow with ease.

Mental/Emotional Structure

The web we build with our thoughts as well as our social connections make up our mental/emotional structure. The tribal group you associate with is part of this, your friends, family, coworkers, neighbors, enemies, television stories, newspapers, everything and everyone you interact with on a mental or emotional level. On a larger scale it includes your nationality and race as it relates to your surroundings.

This structure is pivotal when shifting and healing because since you are so deeply enmeshed in it, a shift is often very scary. For example imagine you worked for a pharmaceutical company who pays you quite well. Financially you are dependent on your job. Your family counts on your paycheck to make house payments, to pay for your children's school, vacations, clothes, etc. What if the company you work for sells medication to manage a condition you have and would like to heal?

Now you are in a mental/emotional structure with some physical dependence.

As soon as you attempt to change this part of your structure your whole web will be affected. It would require you to shift everything. So, if a miracle heals your condition maybe you would no longer feel good about promoting a medication that merely manages it. Maybe this medication even has undesirable side effects. In that case, you may want to give up your job. But your home and finances would be endangered and your family would be unhappy with the effects on them. The question becomes do you want to shift out of your medical condition and heal or would it be easier to continue managing it as best you can to stay within this grid?

Does anything come to your mind when thinking about your mental/emotional structures, which restrict your life force flow? Do you sacrifice yourself in order to energize a temporary structure?

I make sure to go to places and events that inspire me. Right now I am participating in a poetry workshop. Getting feedback on my poetry as well as listening to other people's work energizes me and inspires me to expand. In the past I also belonged to some groups and attended events that left me feeling depleted and exhausted. I went because I knew the people, some moments were fun and I didn't want to lose the social connections. One of these groups promised great networking opportunities, which could have benefitted my work. Every month I talked myself into going to their meetings. Even though it would have been better for me not to attend, I found some reason to remain a part of the group.

One of my issues in life has been wanting to fit in and to be part of a group. This became more important to me than feeling energized and inspired. I thought if I could fit myself into this structure, the structure would eventually work for me.

Needless to say, these gatherings never amounted to anything and were not good for my business or anything else. They were not bad either, just not inspiring and time consuming.

It took me a long time to become aware of this structure and how it affected me. My kids asked me every time I left for a meeting "why are you going?" Finally I asked myself and discovered I couldn't come up with a positive reason. I cancelled my membership and freed up the time previously spent with the group as well as the time I spend thinking about attending the mandatory meetings. Almost immediately my business opportunities started to come in from other areas. The truth was opportunities couldn't have come from this group because I felt low in life-force-energy when within the structure of the group.

The moment I left the structure, I opened the doors to new possibilities. The nice thing was I was able to maintain a connection with the people I chose from the group without remaining in the confines of it. I make it a rule now to ask myself "why?" before I go anywhere. This doesn't mean that I only do things that are fun, although I try to. It means that whenever I can, I choose to do things that support the most possible life force flow. And often these things are more difficult, because to expand, one has to stretch and grow. I welcome the stretching because it leads to a structure with increased flow of life-force-energy. I also never worry about not being challenged enough, life has a way of adding the challenges to help us grow without any help or planning on our part.

Spiritual Structure

The spiritual web deals with belief systems. We all have belief systems, even if it is the belief that we don't believe in anything. Believing in science and what it can do for us is just as powerful as believing in religion. There is no judgment here as to what belief system you have; the purpose is to become aware

18

of it and see how it affects your life, and how deeply it connects with everything you do. For example, if you believe that no matter what happens, things will work out for you somehow, you will be open to many possibilities when in a situation of despair.

There is no roadmap to belief; it is something you must find within yourself. Your belief system is the strongest structure and to move against your own grain is not only stressful, but most likely will also not have a lasting effect. We are continuously creating evidence, stories and proof to support our belief systems. This is our constant focus.

What are some of your belief structures?
Here are some examples of common belief structures. You have to suffer to succeed. You are born a sinner and can never be truly good. If you do a good job you will be appreciated. Teenagers often believe that they are invincible. Life is hard. I am not relationship material. No one is going to love me. People like me don't become CEO's. I am too old to do.... No one wants to hire someone over 50, etc.

One of the first things I suggest when something happens that challenges ingrained belief structures, is to start collecting evidence of other possibilities. Look around yourself and see if there are people who had the same kinds of issues. Find out how they have solved them. Or if you believe that you have to suffer to achieve certain things in life, collect stories of people who have achieved those very things without suffering. If you believe you are too old to get a good job, collect evidence of older people who have gotten good jobs. Create evidence that supports you're looking in the direction of your goal.

Our belief systems can also affect and sometimes limit our healthcare. I grew up believing in Western, Eastern, Natural, Herbal, Homeopathic, Energetic and Spiritual Medicine. When I get sick I look at all possibilities and decide which will be the most helpful and congruent with myself and my particular condition. In this way my belief system is open and does not restrict me to just one approach. Since the same energy flows through all things, remember that when you judge things outside your belief system you limit yourself.

Do you believe in spiritual healing being the only answer to your condition? Can you look at how Western or Eastern medicine has helped people with that same condition? Or do you only believe in Western medicine? Are there Eastern remedies that address your condition?

Infrastructure

Here is where it all comes together, the different grids are intertwined and cannot be separated from one another. We are multifaceted creatures and all aspects of life work together within each of us. This is your story, your creative web in which you move around. An infrastructure can either be supportive, destructive or sometimes even both simultaneously. Let's go back to the spider web. While the web is supportive for the spider attracting all it needs for its survival, it is deadly for the fly, which is trapped in it. And in our own grids, our webs, we are both spider and fly, we hold both aspects simultaneously. It doesn't matter whether we constructed the grids in our life or were born into them.

Understanding structures is a helpful tool. If you are in a tall building it is helpful to know where the staircases and rooms are. It will help you move around more efficiently. This is the same with the structures of your life. Becoming aware of the structure and infrastructure makes it easier to shift and move around. As I have mentioned earlier, structures don't give life they contain life. A corpse has the same physical structure and grid as a living body, it is the life-force-energy that moves within the structures that gives it life. With this life-force-energy we can decide where to put more or less energy and where to focus creativity for change and rebuilding. If you know the limits and capabilities of your physical, mental and spiritual structures, you can navigate easier on the ocean of life. Life is motion, no moment is the same, it is constantly flowing and changing. Embrace this and become a good swimmer in the ocean of your own life.

Chapter 2

Flow Versus Control

Energy must flow, it cannot be stagnant and stay alive. When we try to control our world or our lives, we are going against the nature of being. Only our structures are rigid and beg for control. But life is a mystery. We do not know what will happen tomorrow or the next moment and we don't even know if we will be here to enjoy it. We often get caught up in trying to predict the future and acting according to the most possible control we can get.

Big industries have been created around control. The insurance industry tells us that we will be fine and taken care of if we subscribe. Wall Street analysts try to predict the future and so do psychics. The information obtained may be right or wrong but the important thing is that no matter how much security and control we seek or pretend to hold, that kind of security is nothing but illusion. Now I am not recommending you cancel your retirement fund and insurance, they are helpful structures just like homes are good shelters, but they are not dependable, they are temporary. What I am asking you to do is to see it for what it is: a good tool.

When people come to me and say they want security, I recommend they move into the highest security prison they can find. It is the most predictable environment to live in. But even there, they would be unprotected from natural disasters, illness or death. Plus I doubt that any of you want to spend the rest of your lives in that kind of environment.

What is constant, what is predictable is the flow of motion. How it will flow and where it will flow, we don't know. But that it will flow is guaranteed. Imagine you are watching water, tar and light flow over a distance towards you. Immediately you know which will reach you first according to how fast each one moves. Light is by far faster than the others and water is still much faster than heavy tar. Life-force-energy is also affected by its consistency. The lighter we keep things, the easier it is to flow. I always recommend a good sense of humor and not to take yourself too seriously. I am sure you have heard the saying that *laughter is the best medicine*. That is because energy flows fast when we laugh.

There is so much more to the universe than we know and understand, it is always expanding and challenging us with new riddles to solve and things to discover. Because of life's unknowns it has been my experience that the universe always has the upper hand. When I am dead set on an answer or have an unwavering opinion, something often happens to challenge that answer, that viewpoint, or outlook. And in the end, it is not the answer or point of view but the ever-expanding movement forward that makes life worth living. Challenges present themselves to propel us forward and keep us alive.

If you were on a beautiful tropical island, enjoying everything you could possibly want and a voice inside you told you to get up and do something that would cause you discomfort and challenge your core, you would ignore it, or at best say I will do it later. But what if moments later a hurricane approaches and shakes you out of your comfort and you are faced with challenges? Instantly you become much more open and listen to that voice for possible solutions. This is the universe's way of nudging us forward, giving us the opportunity to shift. And the truth is, there is no way to control the nature of flow. The only control you have is how well you navigate it.

I live near the Pacific, which has taught me a great deal about navigating the ocean of life. I enjoy playing in the water whenever I have the time and the temperature is comfortable enough for me. Some days the waves are big and scary, with dangerous currents and rip tides and sometimes the water is relaxing and calm. Just like life. So here is how I apply my lessons from the ocean into my life:

In the ocean: Never swim against a rip tide, it will exhaust you and you will eventually drown and get carried out into the vast ocean.

In life: When caught in an intense current of events and demands, don't exhaust yourself going against it. Instead move diagonally until you are out of the current. Then move in the direction you desire.

In the ocean: When a wave approaches there are several options. If it is surfable and you are in the right position for it, you can let the wave carry you in fun, speed and exhilaration across the water.

If you are not in the right position to surf, depending on where you are, you can gently flow above it or, if the wave is breaking, you can dive under it.

In life: If the time and the momentum is right, jump on board and ride the wave of your life adventure.

If the moment is not right, know when to let it pass and wait for the right time.

In the ocean: If the wave is very big and threatens to smash you around, you can roll into a ball and let it tumble you like tumbleweed without doing you any harm. If you fight against it and flag your arms and legs around, the wave will smash you in the ground and get the better of you.

In life: When it feels like a wave of events is crashing down and there is no way for you to get immediate control of the situation, it is best to roll into a ball until the wave has crashed. Then respond to everything without panic and adjust your perspective to the new situation.

In the ocean and in life: The motion of the water cannot be stopped or controlled. How we deal and respond to the motion will affect the outcome of any situation.

To summarize, everything is easier when we flow with the situations at hand. And while the universe will constantly ask us to expand, luckily sometimes it will do so in a humorous way as the following story shows.

The Universe Has A Sense Of Humor

A few years ago while living in Los Angeles I was teaching workshops on intuition, psychic development and prosperity. I planned to teach a Saturday intuition workshop in San Francisco. Up until that point, I had been mostly a stay at home mom. After 9 years this was to be the first weekend away from my children. Schedules checked, lists written, all seemed to be in order, except for the fact that no one had responded to my flier announcing my Saturday workshop. The only people that had registered were from my mailing list, not enough to pay for the venue. My friends and promoters had hung the fliers all over the city and everyone was surprised that there had been no response.

Oh well, I canceled the workshop and accepted a friend's invitation to the opera instead. I really needed time away and looked forward to experiencing myself as someone other than a mother. My friend Jennifer was away that weekend and let me stay in her apartment. She had even let me use her local phone number for the flier. I wound up having a great weekend seeing old friends and walking around San Francisco without strollers, bags of toys, extra emergency clothes and whatever else one needs to keep kids happy on an outing.

Sunday evening, after I returned home from San Francisco I wanted to thank Jennifer for her help and for letting me stay at her beautiful place. I couldn't find my address book. Never mind, I thought, her number is on the flier, along with my name and a photograph of me. So I grabbed a flier and dialed the number. The phone rang only once when a sexy voice answered: Hello you reached the triple X erotic bunny farm, your credit card please. I hung up, dialed again and again.

It turned out I had my face and name on a flier all over San Francisco with the phone number for the triple X erotic bunny farm. I searched for my address book and the email conversations with Jennifer about my flier. There it was, I had made a mistake on one digit in the number. In my initial panic I called another friend and told her what happened. Well you may have guessed, she laughed so hard she could barely talk. I called someone else and got the same reaction. Finally I started laughing. In the days that followed, the story made its rounds in my community bringing joy and laughter to many. I ended with more clients and names on my mailing list through the story than I would have by teaching a workshop that weekend, not to mention the joy I spread.

Initially I felt so embarrassed that I thought I would never teach another workshop and certainly not in San Francisco. Thanks to my friends, I was able to see the humor in the situation, well it would have been difficult not to, with all that laughing going on. I always knew the Universe has a sense of

27

humor. I also understood that if I can manage to see the things that happen in my life with humor, life moves with ease. I allowed the flow of events instead of stopping them and had a great time in the process. Light travels lightly, allow your life force energy to travel lightly too.

Chapter 3

Desire To Improve, Shift, Change And Heal

The desire to improve any kind of situation is part of the motion and expansion of the universe. If you feel the desire for change you are at the starting point of a shift in your life. Perhaps you have become aware of something that could improve. Whether it's a physical, mental, emotional or spiritual situation, you have determined that something could be better. This means that there is space to grow into. It is as if you discovered a window to your room, and by looking out, became aware of life outside your room. New possibilities and adventures await you.

Do you want to heal, improve or change anything in your life? Your health, your job, your living situation, your friends, even the color of your room.
Take a moment to think about what it is that you would like to change?

29

You can write it down or just think about it as you read.

Life is a cycle of hypothesis (desire), thesis (possibility), antithesis (current experience), synthesis (new situation) and then we create proof (new experiences). We have an idea how we desire to live, and in contrast we observe how we live. We then see how others live closer to what we desire and form a conclusion about how this could work in our life. Then we shift, adjust and create evidence of new ways to live, by observation and change. It often takes a while because we are strongly connected to our structure. Even though the desire to improve is there, it is not as strong as the ties we have. There are times when we get a little help from the Universe. A situation can become so bad that shifting is the only way to survive, or the offer of something new becomes so enticing that we can't resist any longer, or nature will wipe out the old situation, creating a clean slate for us.

While many shifts take time and effort, instantaneous and miraculous shifts and healings are definitely possible, but they can be overwhelming. The bigger the shift, the more severe the adjustment will be. Some shifts are so powerful that the person is not able to cope with the new situation right away. In that case, they will grab hold of whatever structure is nearest to them. For example a person can become suddenly religious or leave society and move to a reclusive area.

More often than not, the desire to shift prepares us for the change. And even if the shift appears to be instantaneous we have been transitioning into it for some time. People pilgrimage to the Temple of Healing in Tibet, where many miracles and great shifts have been experienced. While the healing takes place at the temple in one moment, it had been developed by the long trek through harsh and rugged areas. Before setting out for the Temple of Healing there had to be a desire for change. Once the desire became strong enough the journey started. It is through this difficult journey that a seeker will sever ties to many of the grids he or she was attached to. By the time the destination is reached the grids have changed, the space is prepared for the seeker to expand and step into.

The thought of miraculously shifting from one condition to the next might sound exciting and desirable but it is much more sensible to go a little slower and adjust to the change step by step. It doesn't matter if you are sick, if you are in a relationship that no longer works, a work situation that needs changing or if you are on a spiritual quest ready for a new level or dimension, in order to shift you have to release the ties you have to your existing grids.

Try to expand a little bit every day. Move forward into the direction of your desires. If you are driving a car to a new destination, you may have detours, supplies to get, expected and unexpected stops, maybe even some delays, but as you drive look at the road ahead of you. Maybe there are a few seconds spent to look in the review mirror, to see if anything is coming to get you from behind or to glance back at the road you traveled. But unless you want to be in a car crash your main focus needs to be on the road ahead. I can't stress this enough, look where you are going, and let go of the structures that are behind you. If you are not ready to leave for your road trip of life at least start getting ready for it. The longer you are stagnant, the more you atrophy.

There is a questionnaire I use to help clients get clear about their situation and whether or not they really want to improve at this time. I started doing this because I realized that clarity about the situation is helpful and the more factors are known the easier the transition will be. There are always many sides to every story. Everything in our life serves a purpose and the clearer we are about all the elements involved the better we can navigate.

1.Do you want to heal or shift your present situation?

2.If it is a physical issue, what would it feel like if you did not have this physical condition?

3.If it is a situation like work, relationship, living arrangement, etc., what would it feel like if the situation were different?

4.How will your infrastructure change if your condition changes? For example how will your closest relationships change?

5.How does your issue affect your social life?

6.Can you see yourself without this condition or issue and all that is attached to it?

7.How is the condition serving you in your life?

8.Do you want to heal or shift your present condition?

I am sure you noticed that the first and last questions are the same. The first one is usually answered: *of course otherwise I wouldn't be here*, while the last one is answered in a much more thoughtful manner. When you are able to answer the last question with a clear yes, you have passed the tipping point and are on the home stretch of changing, shifting and healing. The questionnaire if answered sincerely will move you from the desire to shift to actively shifting. To explain this I have chosen to add Sam's story.

Sam's Story

Sam is 45 years old and suffers from a painful autoimmune disorder. He is taking all kinds of medications to keep the pain under control. He had been to many doctors and healers, tried out a variety of modalities to help him heal or at least cope better with his condition. I gave him the questionnaire to fill out. He was a little annoyed by the first question. "Isn't that why I am here," he was irritated and doubted that coming to see me was worth it. He was unable to answer the second question because he had no reference point for being without his condition, so he just said *great*. We skipped the third question but when we reached the fourth he became quiet.

He thought about his wife, kids, parents and even co-workers who related to him with this condition, even identified him by it. He said, "I don't know if my wife would still like me if she didn't have to take care of me. It is a big part of her life." His thoughts went from his wife to his job and his relationships with coworkers, to his mother who had always helped him cope with situations and so on.

His attachment became even clearer when he got to the 7th question. He realized how much attention and care he received because of his condition. After a moment of silence he got up and told me he didn't know if he was ready, or if he even wanted to change anymore. He realized how comfortable he was even with the pain.

I had not expected that reaction to my questionnaire. Well it certainly was not good for business I thought at first. But then again, I do not want to string people along in drawn out sessions that go nowhere, and Sam was too attached to his condition to shift at this point.

But Sam was not unchanged. He left with a new awareness and clarity about his situation. The seed for change was planted in his mind. He was no longer ignorant of the fact that he was holding on to his structure and how deeply embedded he was in it. Suddenly he felt uncomfortable accepting attention and help from others.

Only a few days later I received a call from Sam. He told me that he thought his wife might be happier and their relationship had a possibility to improve if he could do more things with her. He wanted to start the work and play with new possibilities.

Sam is now feeling much better and does many things to move into the direction of a new possibility. He has chosen a slower pace and to be more involved in his process. Wisely so, because an instantaneous shift from his illness to wellness would have been too drastic for him.

Becoming clear of what is holding you captive is mostly all you need to leap forward in your life. Sometimes we have things that are holding us back and we may not be ready to let go of them. Relationships, especially when children are involved can be challenging grids to shift out of, but not impossible. Financially supporting grids that provide the illusion of security are also challenging. But in most cases the desire is the first step, clarity the second and the faith and knowing that things can improve, will tip the scale in favor of a real change.

PART II

Structures That Define Us

So now that you have dipped your toes in the water, let's go a little deeper into the structures that contain us. In the following 3 chapters, we will dive into each structure separately, getting a better understanding of their roles. It is important to note that this is primarily for explanatory purposes. Since we are multidimensional beings, we cannot truly be understood by separating integral parts of a whole, but it will be a good place to start.

Chapter 4

Physical Structure

The physical structure can be broken into two basic categories. In one category we have our bodies, the physical construct that houses our life-force-energy, which is essential for us to experience life. And in the other category we have buildings and other physical structures, which are tangible places or things we rely on. Buildings, such as the house you live in or the office where you work are not essential to survival. Neither are any of the vehicles you have become dependent on, which makes them the simplest and easiest structures to address.

When it comes to external structures, we automatically believe they are well constructed, made to serve their purpose. We do not generally concern ourselves with what goes into erecting a building or assembling a car. We tend to ignore any of the behind the scenes details. I have to admit that I have no idea how my motor works, but I expect my car to start and drive when I turn it on. I expect it will take me from point A to point B until something goes wrong.

Most people are like I am, paying little, if any attention to these structures. But we suddenly become aware of the details of construction when it rains and there is a leak, a pipe bursts, the electricity is interrupted or an earthquake shakes the foundation or collapses the building. This is when we stop and analyze so that we can make decisions. First we diagnose the problem, and then we start thinking about options. Can we fix it, is it worth it, how much effort would it take and so on.

If it is a lifeless structure, the decision is easier because the entanglement with the structure is far less than the entanglement we experience with our own bodies. Still the loss or break down of a lifeless structure can be painful and scary. What if the money is not there to repair the leaking roof or the damaged foundation? What if it is a house passed down to us by our parents? Is it worth repairing or does it need to be let go of. The wheels start turning to figure out what to do and how to handle the situation, resulting in some kind of decision even if the decision calls for no action at all.

Decisions typically coincide with the attachment to the structure. So for example the less attachment is present, the more objective the decisions will be. But regardless of the level of attachment, every time you are made aware of an external structure, you have received a call to attention. You are being asked to examine your attachment to this structure. If the structure in question is your house, think about how much of your life force and energy should go into this house. A very large house may require a lot of energy, or if you need to borrow money to fix it, it may compromise you financially. When you become aware of your attachments and what the structure represents to you, your decisions will be easier to make.

You may ask yourself these questions to help guide your decision making process:

How important is this structure to me?
Does this structure give me enough joy and happiness to balance the effort it takes to maintain it?
Do my structures work for me or am I working for them?
If I were to die soon, what would my decision be?

A house can easily become a money pit and a drain if one doesn't see the structure clearly. It is important to make these structural decisions from clarity instead of emotional and financial entanglements. The loss of a status symbol, financial security, family memories and embarrassment of having made the wrong decision are all issues that can cloud one's clarity.

Many years ago, I bought a beautiful house from an actor in the movie *The Money Pit*. At the time I was looking for a sense of security, something I assumed I would get from this purchase. It turned out, however, that the house lived up to its link to *The Money Pit* rather than to my expectations. Suffice it to say I learned some important financial lessons through that experience. I am happy to disclose that I no longer own that house but thinking of it always gives me a good chuckle. Who in their right mind would buy a house that is in any way associated with the expression "money pit?"

While mine was only a financial lesson, I have heard stories on the news of people who stay in their homes during wild fires, hurricanes and other structurally threatening situations, sometimes losing their lives for a lifeless structure. I invite you to look at your attachments to buildings, places and things and see how deep your connection and involvement is. After you have looked at it for a while, imagine what it would mean to you if you where no longer here to experience it. Are these external structures what you will remember most from your limited time here on earth?

The body is a much more complex construct. It is also our "earth suit," what we wear in order to experience life. The human body is miraculous, all of its different systems work constantly to keep us alive and functioning. I am always in awe of the magic that takes place within my body. The body is forgiving and, up to a point, it even releases the things we inflict upon it. I certainly have mistreated my body and it still manages to heal itself and function incredibly well. Every morning I wake up feeling grateful for my body and my health and the support I get from it. Just the fact that I can sit here typing away is witness to the miracle of my body functioning. Most of the day, however, I take my body for granted. I am not aware of my heart beating or my lungs breathing, and at night I trust that everything will continue to work as I peacefully sleep.

All the miraculous workings of the body do not change the fact that it is a structure to house our life force. As a side note, some people spend time and money on trying to stop their bodies from changing. The whole rejuvenation industry of face-lifts and other products is designed to stay where you are instead of allowing motion into your life.

Do you remember the movie *Groundhog Day* with Bill Murray? On some level, this is a brilliant parallel for what we strive to do, we want to live the day over and over again forgetting that there is a whole universe of new experiences out there for us to engage in. If we had to live the perfect day over and over it would soon become a nightmare, because we are here to experience a variety of emotions and situations.

Coming back to the physical body, you picked this particular suit because it suits you better than any other. The perfect fit. This structure is with you for your time here on earth and at some point, when it is no longer suitable, you will leave it. We all die and eventually everyone leaves the body structure. But for now, reading this, you are still in it, ready to experience the best life has to offer you.

Take a good look at your most important construct. How well do you treat it? Or should I ask how much do you abuse it? If you love your kids, spouse, pets, family or anything in your life, you probably don't abuse them the way you do your own body. Yet it still shows up for you, forgiving most of what you do to it. When the body sounds an alarm and makes it known that it needs some tender loving care, we often complain instead of stopping in our tracks to pamper and take care of it.

What would happen if the body got tired of this game and said no more? Luckily it takes a lot to get there and because of the forgiving nature of our bodies, working with this structure can be manageable. Here is something to meditate on:

Which situations and attachments have a bearing on your body? Are these attachments beneficial for your body or do they limit and abuse it?

Using Our Bodies To Manipulate – The Language Of Sickness

When I was a child I used to pretend to be sick whenever I didn't want to go to school. I was so good at it that I would actually have a fever for a couple of hours, making my body sick and well again at will. Have you called in sick when you didn't want to do something or face a situation? Have you used your body to manipulate situations? I have not met anyone who has not done this. It is so much easier to say: I didn't finish it because I was sick, or I couldn't come because of the flu than to tell the truth: I didn't want to come or I was too relaxed and lazy to finish the work.

These are small lies that put the focus on the body structure being damaged. But they are powerful and most things start small. Using the body to manipulate others into doing or not doing what you want is common. Here is a cliché with a grain of truth to it: I can't have sex tonight I have a migraine instead of saying I don't want to have sex because you didn't act the way I wanted you to. If the migraine manipulation is

41

used long enough the body will respond with migraines even if you didn't have any at first. If you don't want your body to compromise you, start by not compromising your body. Your relationship to your body is the key to experiencing your life.

Take a moment to allow your body to let you know how you treat it. Make note of the many areas where you can improve the relationship.

Ultimately you are in charge of your relationship, you tell the body what to do. You wouldn't let your house tell you how to live your life, but if you damage your house and you don't take care of it, it will deteriorate and fall apart.

It is the same with the body. It is a structure. Know your structure. See if the body you have chosen can perform the tasks you demand of it or if you need to approach certain tasks differently. Care for your body suit and maintain its parts. The body structure is much more capable of performing miracles than it is given credit for and it renews itself constantly. Every cell in the body restores and renews all the time, but the cells renew according to your present state of affairs. They regenerate according to the current blueprint of patterns and beliefs that you hold. If you can step out of these patterns and grids into the space of Oneness, the body has a chance to renew in line with the blueprint that follows the best possible flow of life force.

Let us say you had an injury that restricts your movement. It is possible to restore to the full range of motion by allowing the parts to go back to their original state of being. In order to do so you may have to let go of your attachments and belief structures, which tell you that this is impossible. Miracles happen. Allow them and look towards your goal. It is exciting to realize that we are not victims of our constructs but the creative force within it, allowing shifts and expansion of life-force. In part three of this book I will explain the structural healing and shifting process in depth.

When a construct has fulfilled its purpose and taken us as far as possible on the journey of experiencing life it is time to move on to the next adventure. There are reports of people that have had glimpses of life after life, but there is no tangible proof. Really, this is no different than anything else we encounter. We never truly know what the next moment will bring. But the veils at the end of physical life seem thicker and therefore more scary. Some cultures are more at peace with this step than others.

In the United States there is a huge attachment to the body and many are kept functioning even long after any desirable quality has gone. At huge costs we keep bodies alive even after the life-force and spirit have abandoned the structure. Today an estimated 25% of all Medicare costs are spent in the last 6 months of life. The following story shows how our choices are sometimes rendered without thinking it through and how they impact the quality of our life.

Abigail's Story

Abigail was a hospice client, who told me on her deathbed that a few months earlier when she became ill she saw an angel in her dream. The angel asked her if she wanted to come now or stay and experience the illness. She looked at the angel and even though the peace emanating from the angel was very inviting she decided to stay.

She told me the decision was made because of all the things she liked to do and the people she was attached to. She never did those things again and suffered a great deal during the months to come. Many times she had hoped the angel would come back. First she was upset, but then she made the best of her situation. During that time she made peace with many people from her past, she welcomed forgiveness and joy. She barely complained about her pain and her caretakers all enjoyed her peaceful and uplifting presence.

When she finally left her body all were sad to see her go. She told to me that she had been so attached to her body and life that she didn't really register the peace and love emanating from the angel. She said she had to slowly come to the realization that she would have to let go of her body and life on her own.

The option to release her attachments was presented to her before the pain and slow deterioration set in. Was her decision to hold on right or wrong? My answer to that is that there is no right or wrong. Abigail went through lots of pain, but she did also have rich experiences in those last months of her life.

Chapter 5

Mental/Emotional Structures

Physical structures are easy to recognize and shift because we can see and interact with them. Mental-emotional structures, on the other hand, are not as easy to identify. Because they are not tangible, they are more illusive than the physical structures, but they tend to be just as strong, if not stronger. How we relate to others and act in situations is just as much of a construct as the body we present or the buildings we enter.

Hi, it is so nice to meet you!

How are you?

What do you do?

Where do you work?

Where do you live?

Do you have kids, a family?

These are some of the first questions we encounter when meeting new people. Try answering these for yourself and you will start to sense many of your mental/ emotional structures.

Now re-answer them all and after each answer, let the questioning teenager in you come out and ask "Why?" The moment you ask the question "Why?" you start becoming aware of your choices. Now it is no longer just a phrase automatically uttered, it becomes a choice. Why do you choose to live where you live? Why do you choose to have or not to have a family? Why do you choose to work where you work? Answering these questions will help you become more conscious of yourself and the structures through which you express yourself on a daily basis.

The closest and easiest mental emotional constructs and webs to recognize are family relationships. From the moment we are conceived, we are exposed to the emotions of the people around us. The chemicals a pregnant mother releases during her daily emotional experiences will affect her fetus and as that fetus develops, what has been passed on by the mother will become a part of the mental/ emotional structure. Once we are born, the people we encounter and the situations we experience will all shape our responses to situations and soon we have a rigid web that directs most of our life.

Think of your parents. They had a certain idea of how your life should be, what decisions you should make, who your friends should be etc. For a while it worked. Their structure became your world. Your life story was guided by the people who were close to you, and your experiences were determined by your caregivers and your immediate environment. Then your life started to expand. You met different kids on the playground, in school or your neighborhood and then finally you became a teenager and started to question if what you had learned so far was right for you.

Through observation and interaction with others, you formed your own grid. This step may have been scary and fun at the same time. You no longer could blame your caregivers, you started to be responsible for your own decisions. Then as an adult you add your profession, work situation, new social surroundings and maybe your own family with children to it. Your children will be introduced to life in your structure.

Throughout life it would be great to keep that wonderful teen attitude of questioning. It is helpful to periodically check if one's decisions are still fitting or if they need to expand. Whenever you observe and question yourself, you instantly open up for more.

Is This All There Is Or Is There More?

According to psychologists, we have an estimated 60,000 thoughts a day and 95% -98% of them are repeated daily. That leaves us with average 2% -5% of new thoughts. Our thoughts dictate our reactions to what is around us.

Instead of wandering in unknown territory we tend to stay with the familiar. It doesn't matter if the situation is positive, challenging, or negative, we react according to the mental emotional structure that holds us. Staying in the same structures and webs can make us feel in charge or in control of life. But not only is that an illusion, it also goes against our expanding flowing nature. If your heart decided to stop beating because it likes where it is and wants to stay there, you would cease to exist in physical form.

The same truth applies here, you are not your constructs, you are the life-force that flows within them. Your life-force wants to expand and it will find ways to do so, by creating events that will challenge the rigidity of your constructs. If you stop the flow and expansion of life-force within one of your structures, that structure will cease to be alive and functioning for you.

It is like a relationship that ceases to exist when the parties involved are no longer present or if one of them is no longer invested in it. If there are many people involved in that relationship it may continue for some time, but if you pulled all your life-force out of it, it would no longer be part of your life. Stagnation of life-force within a structure is similar to pulling your life-force out of the structure. The difference is that moving your life-force into expansion is exhilarating and leaving life-force to stagnate is a painful death. Remember life-force has to flow in order to exist.

Let's take a look at your professional life.
Why do you work where you do?
Do you work to support your surrounding structure: income, home, cars, vacations, social status, etc.?
Do you associate hard work with suffering or with fun?
And if you are currently not employed, you can still ask yourself the above questions of previous employment, employment you are seeking or any occupation or activity linked to your survival.
Why and where are you looking for work?
What kind of work are you looking for?

For example if you dislike your work but you are very attached to your surrounding structure, income, home, cars, vacations, what restaurants you eat in, social circles etc. you will most likely stay in the job that keeps your structure stable, even if it is not good for you. You may even get stress related physical or emotional diseases.

Whatever constructs you have built around your profession is neither right nor wrong, it simply is something to be aware of. Each decision you have made serves a purpose.

My advice when answering the above questions and looking at your work or other emotional / mental structures is to stay as neutral as possible. That way, it is easier to shift. Try to look at these constructs the same way you look at houses. One is going to be more suitable for your needs and wants than others and over time your needs will change. So when the house you have lived in for so many years feels too small or too big, or you simply don't like the neighborhood anymore, take the op-

48

portunity to move and shift. The following story illustrates how life opens up when we let go of outdated structures.

Jake's Story

One of my clients, Jake grew up in a poor family. Everything was about survival, from getting enough to eat to navigating a dangerous neighborhood. His life was a daily fight just to stay alive. His structures were built around survival against the odds. The Universe supplied experiences fitting into his structures: he was drafted into the military and soon found himself in Vietnam fighting for his survival in war. After attending a university, he became a successful businessman.

Still everything he did was underlined by the structure of fighting for whatever he encountered in life. Whether it was beating the competition, fighting for causes or solving homework problems with his kids, he was always up against an invisible enemy who needed to be conquered. At work and at home Jake's operating structure evolved around encountering problems and fighting to solve them. His life was always full of challenges. Easy-going was not how you would describe him or the structure he operated in. He even chose to watch weekly war documentaries as a form of entertainment. His world was rooted in struggle.

During one of our sessions, Jake became aware of this structure in his life. When he talked, he described his life the way other people might describe a war. When talking about issues, both physical and emotional, he often mentioned that he was *attacking* issues, *battling* and *fighting* something or needing to *kill* his headaches. I recorded our conversations and we listened together counting the aggressive words and descriptions. He was surprised when he noticed his own language. But by observing himself and listening to his vocabulary he became aware of his structure.

49

We talked about alternative ways of being and he could soon see the possibility of leaving his life of war and entering a construct where things flowed peacefully and with ease. Needless to say, his transformation and shift were beautiful to watch. And it all began with awareness. Once that awareness is present, everything is ready to shift. Of course, the shifting still has to take place, but it becomes easier when a glimpse of a new possibility appears.

Take some time and write a description about your life as if you were telling someone your story.
Then read it highlighting verbs and adjectives and see if you can recognize any patterns.

The Groups That Define Us

Another part of your web is your cultural and racial background. This construct is strong because there are many people in it, who constantly feed it. Having been born into post World War II Germany, I have been confronted with issues stemming from the NAZI regime many times. Even my children who were born in the United States have been called NAZIs in school, because their mother was born in Germany.

I consider myself very lucky to have come from a family that was part of the underground movement and put me on the "good side". I have also had and used the option to say I was Swedish or Danish to avoid discussion. This is not so easy if you are, for example, African American, Asian or Middle Eastern and your skin color and physical structure place you within the issues of the grids. Even if you are not racist, as an African American in the United States you will certainly be confronted with racism and issues affecting your race.

I think it is one of the more difficult structures to shift. It takes a very strong spirit to simultaneously live within a racist/minority grid and let go of that structure. President Obama for example had to move past the mental structures, which prevented African Americans from becoming President in order to even run for that office.

It doesn't matter whether you are in a racial, political, sexual oriented, majority, minority, victim, bullying or personal preference structure, the key is to become aware of its influence on your behavior. No matter what part of the grid you are attached to, what side you are fighting for, you are operating within the confinements of your structure. Healing and shifting beyond those grids can be done by forgiveness, acceptance and non-judgment. It can only happen when you realize that the same energy and life-force flows through all and everything.

Getting Another View

Part of shifting our existing grids is being able to see alternatives. For example, when we take a vacation we step into a different structure for a while. We are often able to reframe and get a better awareness of our surrounding grids. But it is important to note that reframing, while useful, is not the same as shifting.

In a session, one of my clients told me that he enjoys his tropical vacations so much because he becomes a different person when he is there. He said that when he returns home, as soon as he reaches his local airport, he feels the density of the people and is immediately pulled back into stress and problems. He wishes he could live permanently on the tropical island.

I can relate to his feelings and I think you can too. It is nice to step out of the usual grid and our structures. But the temporary stepping out does not shift our mental and emotional structures. So if he really moved to the island without changing his personal construct, he would, after a short time, encounter the same stress and problems there. Issues can show up in a different backdrop and with new costumes and faces, but the issues of the challenges will be the same. Don't let this stop you from going to fun places. Leaving the structure and grid of daily life is useful for collecting possibilities.

Think of a vacation you have taken recently.
Did the different structure inspire you? How?
What shifts, if any, can you make in your life to incorporate that experience?

Always observe yourself and then take action. The more aware you are of your structure the easier it will become to move out of it and to create a new, more evolved structure. Observe yourself and observe what motivates your decisions. Use your 2% -5% of new thoughts a day to move into the direction of expansion. There is always room to expand.

Chapter 6

Spiritual Structures And Belief Systems

Spiritual structures, grids and belief systems are the most rigid and hardest to evolve. As everything else around them is changing, expanding and evolving, they tend to remain fixed. Belief systems hold within them the attitude of *I am right*, which by nature declares all others wrong.

You could probably think of all the people you know that hold on to their beliefs even though you think their belief structure doesn't make sense or can't be right. They probably think the same about you.

Because regardless of what belief system one holds, even if it is the belief in nothing, science, Darwin, religion, aliens, reptilians, enlightenment, atheism, etc. this structure serves as our main operating system. The construct of belief determines how we approach all issues in life. Therefore if something comes along that challenges our belief to expand and evolve we become very resistant.

This is our core and we are prepared to defend it no matter what. Just think how many wars have been fought on behalf of spiritual and belief systems. It must be easier to fight than to shift.

History and politics even today give evidence to how strong these grids are. We see on a daily basis how many people are killed on behalf of religious belief systems, even when the religions themselves seem to condemn such behavior. The commandment "Thou shalt not kill", Exodus 20:13, has not prevented the genocide of indigenous people in South America or the crusades, etc.

If everyone could recognize beliefs as constructs for unified life-force to move through, there would be no more wars. We would realize that we are all the same essence flowing within different structures. My goal in this book is to help you take a look at your own belief systems as an observer and without judgment. That will ultimately be the best way for you to figure out where you are within your grids and determine your personal modus operandi.

Not all belief systems are as easily recognized as religious structures. A spiritual structure includes everything you believe in. This can be a certain political system, a street gang, medical science, family and friends, support systems of any kind, nature, nurture, etc. Because these are all so deeply ingrained, a shift in spiritual structure usually takes a big jolt. Financial ruin, accidents, natural disasters, or other big events can cause a jolt like this.

There are numerous books and stories about people who had near death experiences and how the experience completely changed their lives. Many people who encounter a shift of that magnitude change not only their spiritual structures but all the other ones as well. If all of a sudden you become clairvoyant some people might think you have gone crazy, or if you were an atheist who now sees angels, your new state will shift how your old friends relate to you. Of course you have the option to keep your new abilities quiet and not let people know. That means your shift happened only in some of the structures and you are choosing the gentle approach versus the jolt.

As a child I saw things that were not visible to others around me. I kept it to myself because I was afraid of losing all my friends. Later in my teens I pretended to do hallucinatory drugs to fit in, but I never actually did any. I could barely manage what I saw without them. Most of the time I saw people's emotions in the form of pictures, or animals superimposed on them. So I was grateful for the sixties. I could blend in. It took years for me to be open about my abilities. When I did open up, things changed but they changed at a pace that I could handle.

How Beliefs Shift

You constantly weigh your belief in contrast to other belief systems, by either rejecting them or contemplating their truth. After enough evidence supports the new belief, the tipping point is reached and the scale will favor the new belief. This can take a long time but once the scale tips the new system is in place. People used to believe that the earth was flat. That belief continued until someone challenged it and tried to reach the end of the earth and the end of the belief as well.

Let's say you don't believe in instantaneous, spiritual healing. Faced with a terminal disease you are in the hospital hooked up to machines waiting for death. Moments later with no explanation you are well and there is no sign of your disease. This experience will tip your scale.

Beliefs are everywhere, dietary beliefs, having to struggle to succeed beliefs, how kids should be raised beliefs, people don't like me, people of different ethnicity don't like me, God is judging my actions, etc. Anytime you have an opinion about anything it is backed by your belief system, even small opinions like nonfat milk is better than whole milk is a belief system.

I know you are aware of the major belief systems and structures in your life and if you are like most of us you have set up an auto pilot system to guide you. For the most part it probably worked well, but if you have picked up this book you are at a point where you desire some shift. Either you wish to expand or you are faced with a challenge or emergency demanding a shift.

So let's start by introducing you to yourself the way we might address someone we really wanted to get to know: "Hi, so nice to meet you! What do you believe in?"

(Of course this intro is really only reserved for you. I don't recommend using this line at a party or on a first date.)

So, what do you believe in? Here are some questions to ask yourself in your daily life to gain clarity. Again, remember there is no right or wrong answer.

Make a list of some of your most recent decisions. They could range anywhere from choosing to get a divorce to deciding what kind of milk to buy. Now ask yourself the following questions:
What percentage of my decision/action is based on:
Religious beliefs?
Cultural traditions?
Other people's opinions?
Common beliefs?
Fear of the unknown?
Is it structure or the flow of life-force that drove my decision/action?
Am I going in the direction of expansion?

The wonderful thing about being here on earth is that everyone is operating from their own structures and therefore appears different. Every day we are confronted with others who have different spiritual structures. We are shown other ways to operate and we are given the opportunity to integrate a new addition to our present grids, or to completely shift into an expanded one.

PART III

How To Heal And Shift

"No Problem can be solved by the consciousness that created it." *Albert Einstein*

Shifting consciousness is the key to solving or healing anything. This shift of consciousness doesn't even have to be a permanent one. If you can just manage for a split second to step into a different mindset, you can access other possibilities, find the elusive answer, or experience the much needed healing. You may feel that this is easier said than done, but I assure you it can be easy or difficult, the choice is yours.

When you review your past and the significant changes you have made, you will notice how fast you actually shifted. What made it seem difficult was your grip on the consciousness that created the problem. What made it take a long time was your inability to let that consciousness go.

Normally, if there is something within screaming for expansion or change, it will show up in one or all of the structures as well as the infrastructure of life. The scream will be as loud as necessary and come from the part of you that will bring you to your knees and mandate that you listen. This differs for each of us. Some people stop and pay attention when they encounter physical pain, some with financial pain and others through emotional or spiritual pain. When the call to attention comes, it is time to shift, adjust and improve your structures to allow life-force to flow easier.

Your energy automatically feeds your focus. Whatever you feed will grow, whether it is pain or well-being. As you read, think about where your focus lies.

Chapter 7

Shifting The Physical Structure:
Shifting Out Of Pain

What part of your body hurts?
How did that part of you feel before it started to hurt?
How does that part of your body feel without pain?
If you don't know ask yourself: If I knew, what would it feel like?

If you experience pain and would like to be pain free, you have to step from a space of pain into a space of feeling well, a space that you probably are not familiar with because you've never paid attention to it. Pain demands your attention. In order to shift out of pain, it is helpful to know the space of feeling no pain, of just being. The more intense the pain, the more attention it demands, the more challenging it will be to focus on well-being.

Most everything in our bodies is taken for granted and expected to perform without conscious input. The moment something happens that causes pain, the awareness jumps to that discomfort. For example, I rarely think of my teeth unless I am taking care of their hygiene and maintenance. They are just there. I use my teeth all the time without giving them any attention. All of a sudden I have a toothache. Now all of my thoughts are focused on my teeth. My daily routine and plans change to make room for an appointment with my dentist. As soon as he fixes the problem, I go back to my normal way of being and soon any awareness of my teeth disappears again. I don't feel my teeth unless they hurt. If you would ask me in the midst of a toothache how my teeth feel when they are not hurting, I wouldn't know.

When in a state of pain, the question is how can I move from this state to one of well-being? How can I become free of the pain and the symptoms that caused it? Earlier I used the metaphor of the house and it fits here as well. When a house is engulfed in flames, the first thing to do is to put out the fire without any question.

After that is accomplished, the damage can be assessed and plans for repair or rebuilding can get underway. When the fire is raging it is not the time to sit and meditate and hope that things will get better, unless you have mastered the art of commanding nature and are capable of stopping the fire with your mind alone. For most of us this is not the case.

Now, once you have addressed the flames and the fire is put out, the house needs to be rebuilt. You are not going to want to live among that ashes and broken glass. So you create a new vision of the newly renovated house. Maybe you even make some improvements and take care of it in a way that would prevent a similar fire from happening. If you want a nice house to live in you look forward to the repairs and put your energy into the end result, a nice home. Another option would be to remain in mourning for all that is lost and the fact that you will never have a nice place again etc. you may move into the surviving shed and look at your ruins every day.

But let's go back to the house on fire, or the body in pain. It is important to keep your focus on the road ahead. Not in a daydream, but right in front of you, so that you move in the direction you wish to move in without crashing.

When the house is burning, you put out the fire. When pain strikes, you tend to the immediate needs, and then you look at the road ahead, the one leading to your goal of well-being.

With the house, even after the fire is extinguished, it is not effective to muse about the cigarette that was burning or the stove that was on, or whatever started the fire. You can find out what caused it to prevent it from happening again, but then move forward. Blaming what or who caused the fire does not undo any damage. It only causes additional misery. The same goes for physical pain. First you need to address the pain or injury, and then quickly examine what caused it to get the necessary information to avoid repetition, and then move in the direction of well-being.

Here are some tools to put out the fire and to rebuild the house, once the fire has been extinguished:

Visualize Well-Being

Pain hogs your attention. It can be difficult to focus on well-being when in an acute state of pain. And there is another issue. If you focus on being without pain or pain free, your focus will still be on pain. The mind cannot process negatives without activating them. For example, right now please don't, under any circumstances, whatever happens, do not, I am serious, do not think of a pink elephant – – what happened? I asked you not to think of a pink elephant! I know, you still thought of a pink elephant. It is the same with pain. In order to focus on a state of being pain free you have to create something that doesn't refer to the word pain.

You can think of well-being, or create a symbol that signifies the state you want to move into. Find a word, a sound, an image of well-being, which you can focus on, a symbol that has no connection to pain. Use this symbol as a focal point and concentrate on it as often as possible.

Get Support

You are not alone, help is available everywhere. Find yourself a healer, doctor or practitioner of your choice who can hold the space of well-being for you if you can't do it yourself because you are in the crisis. But remember nobody else can heal you, you have to do the healing yourself. Medications and doctors or healers can only guide and assist you and they can hold the door for you so the shift is easier.

Unfortunately the medical field is focused more on what is wrong than on what is right. This negative focus will hold you back. If you are aware of this you can steer the focus from what is wrong to well-being. Something else that frequently holds us back is denial. Denial is a temporary space and when you become aware of it, leave it as fast as you can. The alarms will only get louder and louder until you can hear them.

It is best to be conscious and aware of your body structure, listen to the pain, look at what needs attention, take the measure you see fit, seek the help and advice that you are comfortable and congruent with and shift your focus toward your goal of well-being.

Practice Gratitude

A good preventative activity in times of well-being is to become aware of yourself, your body, its magnificence, its incredible intricate workings and appreciate it. Be grateful for your organs and limbs, love yourself and all your parts. Pick at least one part of your body each day to focus on with gratitude and appreciation, become familiar with the feeling of well-being and well-functioning in your whole body. Doing this will help you in situations of crisis and is essential to regain well-being.

Separate Structure From Being

What happens if you don't know the space of well-being? Remember in the beginning when we talked about structure? Pain is an experience you can encounter because you move within your body structure. It is not you. You are the life-force, the space of Oneness. This space of Oneness always knows everything there is to know.

When you move from the illusion that you are your structure to the reality of being Oneness, all answers and all possibilities become available. These answers can show up anywhere in your life, as a friend, a vision, a doctor, a healer, an inner knowing, etc., because in this space of Oneness we are all connected.

The following stories show how you can either guide yourself to move toward healing the physical body, to shift into healing, or how you can slow down the process and remain where you are.

Bill's And Sara's Story

Bill came to one of my seminars with arthritis pain. He had been in pain for about 5 years. When I asked him if he could remember how he felt 10 years ago he answered "Great. I played basketball with my son in the evening and I felt good."

I asked Bill to step into that memory of playing basketball, and having a blast. He closed his eyes and imagined it. While he stood there with a big grin on his face, I asked him to remind his joints of the feelings he experienced back then and to let them know what exactly it was they felt and did. How did his anatomy function as he dunked the ball into the net and high fived his son. I then told him to tell his body to do the same thing right now. At the same time, I asked him to let go of his mind and thoughts and enter into the space of Oneness, like falling into the arms of love. Safe and protected I asked him to release all his thoughts and ideas, letting go of structure and what he knew about it. After a few seconds I asked him how he felt. He still had the grin on his face and as he moved his body around. He noticed that the pain was gone.

My only advice for him was to keep moving forward into the direction he wanted to go, looking for more and more moments of feeling great. Bill created a new focal point for himself, a focal point of his joints moving with ease and joy and the possibility of moving from pain to well-being within seconds. He knew what to do.

Bill's experience is common. Many people experience the shift out of pain or other restrictions, when reminded to do so during sessions or in seminars. Bill was able to take his instantaneous shift and continue to move in the direction of well-being. Bill did not look back and even when someone asked him how he thought his healing shift happened he answered: "I don't care how or what happened, I am having a great time feeling fantastic, that is all I need."

Sara had the same issue. After a similar exercise she kept moving her wrists around looking to find some pain and then said: "Of course, when I am here with you I feel so relaxed that the pain diminishes. It is just about relaxation, so when I return to my daily life the pain will be back."

Let's look at Sara's situation. Yes, she is right, relaxation will reduce the experience of pain because more flow is possible when we are relaxed. Pain is like stress, it is tense in nature, therefore relaxation will reduce it. But Sara's focus remained on being in pain even while not in pain.

As I mentioned before, we will always move in the direction of our focus. Therefore if you are focused on the pain, it is very likely that the painful condition will return.

So while Sara's body shifted out of pain during a session, her other structures remained centered around her condition of pain, the scale still weighing heavily on the pain side. She was actually looking for the pain. However, even though Sara was not able to shift her structures at that moment, she was introduced to a new reference point of possibilities. And this new point will slowly nudge her in the direction of healing.

When the flow of life-force through your body structure is in need of expanding, it will let you know. How you respond to it is up to you. If you pay attention to the little aches and respond lovingly toward your structure, you can probably avoid a lot of misery.

Take a moment to check in with your body and listen to it.
Is there something you can do to improve your well-being?
Where is your focus?
Are you focused on being well?
Are you focused on the pain and on what is wrong?

Another big part of shifting out of pain lies in the way you emotionally respond to the pain. When your body is in pain, it is asking you to take care of something. Often we respond with anger, or wanting to disown the part of the body that is in pain. Imagine your body as an external person, someone you depend on for your life, someone you care about and love more than anything. If this other person had an accident or got sick and was in terrible pain how would you respond? Would you want nothing to do with them anymore? Would you get angry because the person is sick and needs you?

Your body is the structure you need to experience life, yet most of us don't treat it with love.

When I was a child I had an infected finger from a cactus thorn. First it hurt a little but I ignored it. All of a sudden the pain became intense and unbearable. I cried and told my dad that I wanted the finger off. We were on vacation at the time and my dad decided to take me to the hospital. My whole finger was badly infected.

On the way to the hospital he told me to think about all the things I need the finger for, like playing the piano and other instruments. Also, he reminded me, it would be more difficult to write and draw without it. Then he asked me if I was my finger, how would I feel if someone told me: since you are in pain, I don't want you anymore, I am just going to chop you off. Would you like to cooperate with this person? Would you like to get better to be with this person? Of course I wanted to keep my finger and I started apologizing to my finger on the way to the doctor. Today all that is left from that incident is a small scar and a huge lesson I apply again and again.

The other morning I woke up with burning pain in my leg. I could feel my femur as if it were on fire. The pain was so intense that it brought tears to my eyes. I lay in my bed and thought: I love my leg. I concentrated on the beautiful walks I take on the beach and all the other amazing things I do together with my leg. "I love my leg, I am so grateful for all the support you have given me, is there anything I can do for you to make you feel better?" became my mantra.

I went to the doctor who recommended cortisone shots to get rid of the pain. When I asked what was wrong he wasn't certain but he thought this would work and make me feel better. I am not fond of injections and I didn't want to treat myself on a trial and error basis. I told him I would think about it and went home to lie in my bed with tears and my mantra. I stayed in bed all day loving my leg.

Eventually I fell asleep again. I woke up at 2:15am and there was no pain. I jumped out of bed landing on both my legs dancing around feeling great, appreciating my legs, especially the right one.

What was wrong? What made it better? I don't have an answer for you, the only thing I know is that I didn't turn against my body at a time of need. I embraced and loved it, while focusing on the result I wished for.

Here are a few things to remember:
If you focus on pain you energize it.
Pain is an attention hogger.
If you can't focus on being free of pain while you are in pain, find someone who can help you hold the space of well-being for you.
If you want your body to work with you treat it as best you can. Inundate it with love and gratitude.

Chapter 8

Shifting Emotional Structure:
Shifting Out Of Pain And Into Love

Before you begin this chapter, think of the person or animal that you love the most. This could be your partner, child, favorite pet, relative or friend. Let the image of this being become clear in your mind's eye and allow the love you feel for them to fill you completely. Once you have conjured up this being and the love you feel for them, you may let their image recede to the back of your mind, as we will return to this thought later on.

Emotional pain is always connected to love. In order to heal or shift out of emotional pain, we must understand what love is and how love moves in our lives.

Without love we do not exist. Take a look at the story of your life and other people's lives throughout history. If you look closely you will see that everything in life is about love and that every story is essentially a love story. It is either about receiving, giving, withdrawing, promising, withholding, wanting, needing, experiencing, or losing love. Love is the same energy as life-force energy. The closest we can get to experience ourselves as pure life-force-energy is through the emotion of love. Love is the most powerful, emotional, wonderful experience, and it is what everyone seeks. Show me how you love and I show you who you are.

When you experience emotional pain you are experiencing the loss of feeling love. While the reality is that love never does abandon us, the illusion of structure and separation here on earth can feel like a loss of love. In order to heal this kind of emotional pain, you need to learn how to step back into the love that you think you lost. The best and fastest way to achieve this is through self-love.

Dealing with emotional pain is unlike confronting physical pain, where we have a first aid kit and can spring into immediate action to fix what is wrong or at least stop the bleeding.

When we encounter emotional pain, tools are not always at our fingertips. There are some immediate physical reactions to help us cope. Tears for example are a natural release mechanism. But what if we are in a situation were we feel uncomfortable if someone sees us cry? In that case we may block our natural response tool. In addition to the release of tears, the body produces chemicals to help deal with certain situations. In the severest cases, a temporary numbness or shock can set in. In less severe cases there is still a release of endorphins into the system to help cope with the given situation.

Emotional pain is just as powerful as physical pain and, when held inside or denied, will exacerbate the existing pain or even create new pain. This new pain can be in the form of emotional, psychological or even physical diseases. To avoid an even more severe emotional injury, it is vital that we tend to our injuries immediately just like we would a broken leg, a wound etc. The first step is to take care of the injury as soon as it occurs. Unfortunately, that is rarely what we do.

As a matter of fact, many people do the exact opposite: they add physical injury to the emotional one. I have seen many people punch objects or even hit their heads against walls when suffering emotionally. Some people respond by eating large amounts of unhealthy foods, causing them to become overweight or obese. Of course the ultimate form of hurting yourself when in a state of emotional pain is suicide. So, why is it so common to inflict more self-pain when undergoing emotional pain?

Let's take a look at the reasons. Let's say someone has hurt your feelings. You are hurt and you don't know how to apply emotional first aid, but you do know how to apply physical first aid. You move the pain from the emotional plane onto the physical one because now it is tangible and visible and you know what to do. Another reason is that if you were hurt by someone, that person can now literally see what they have done to you, and hopefully will feel bad about it. Maybe if your injury is severe enough they will come back and give you the love that you thought you had lost.

I have had several clients who thought about or even attempted suicide with the desire to force their partners not to leave them. Of course this is extreme but not uncommon.

How have you dealt with emotional injury in the past?
Have you used physical injury of any kind to manipulate the situation that caused the pain?

Taking the emotions out of it for a moment, let's look at the situation logically. It really does not make sense to hurt yourself because you are hurt. This behavior does not help diminish emotional pain, it only adds physical pain to the emotional pain. You and your body should be each other's most treasured friends and closest allies.

71

If you saw someone lying in the street in pain, would you walk over to hurt that person even more simply because he or she is already hurt? Probably not. I think you would even try to help in any way possible. Then why would you treat a person you don't even know better than you would treat yourself? It does not make any sense. Remember the person I asked you to visualize in the beginning of this Chapter? The one you care about most? Imagine that person has been emotionally hurt by someone or by an event. How do you react? Do you go over and punch them, or hit their head, or try to kill them? I think you will love and support them in any way you can, assuring them that you are there to help. If that person is crying you most likely will put your arms around them and whisper that you are here for them.

And this is exactly what you should do for yourself! Next time you are in a situation where you are emotionally injured, think of what you would do if your favorite person were in this situation and apply that to yourself. Pamper yourself, love yourself, hold yourself in your arms and take care of yourself. If the pain is so strong that you can't see or grasp the state of no pain or less pain, find someone who can help you and hold that space of well-being for you.

When my son was 4 years old I picked him up from pre-school. Not long after he had gotten in the car he started crying. I pulled over immediately thinking that he had gotten hurt. I checked for injuries or bruises. He cried so hard that he couldn't speak. I took him in my arms and rocked him until he calmed down. Finally between sobs he uttered "my feelings are hurt". I continued to hold him, assured him that I was there for him, that I loved him. Later when he felt better, we were able to talk about what had happened and I could continue to support him.

I like this moment because it illustrates how you should treat yourself when you encounter emotional pain.

Acknowledge the pain, be your own best friend and get the support you need.

When you encounter a specific emotional injury for the first time like the first heartbreak or the death of a loved one, it feels more severe, because you don't know that you can survive it yet. There is no evidence of a happy ending or a guarantee that life will continue and get better again. Until you have survived an emotional injury it is useful to look at other people who have gone through similar injuries, talk to friends, get help, attend a support group. Collect evidence for yourself, which shows that things can improve and will get better. Doing this will enable you to focus on a reference point of well-being.

Here are the three basic steps to healing emotional pain:

Question: What happened, what caused the pain?
Allow: Allow the pain, don't deny or ignore it!
Love: Tend to yourself and move into the direction of love.

Love Versus Attention

We search for love constantly. When a person feels that love is out of reach, they will often reach for attention, which is also a form of energy but no substitution for love. Attention is a temporary energy that fuels our structures for a limited amount of time. Like the gas you put in your car, it will allow you to go only a certain distance until you need to secure more.

Often attention is extracted via negative behavior. I used to work in early childhood education and I noticed when working with children that if they didn't receive enough loving attention, they would quickly resort to behaviors that would get them any kind of attention. There were kids that would get hurt and others that would do things that were against the rules and get scolded, because, after all, if someone was scolding them, someone was paying attention. But you cannot replace love with attention. They are two different things.

Love is the experience of flow of life-force, attention is an expression bestowed on something of importance. Attention is interest in something important or relevant in that moment. Love is importance regardless of circumstance. When you love someone, they are important to you and you pay attention to them because of their place in your heart. When you are merely giving someone attention, the reason could be that they are particularly interesting or what they are doing may be affecting you. You are paying attention to them because they are in your path.

It can be easy to confuse attention stemming from love with attention for attention's sake. They both create that sense of feeling cared about and being a priority. The problem is, that extracted attention feeds the ego. As long as the attention flows, the ego is pleased. When attention becomes stagnant, situations demanding attention can be consciously or even unconsciously generated.

For example a woman hurts herself because her spouse has had an affair. When she found out that her husband had an affair she felt the loss of attention, immediately she went into hurting herself to demand his attention to be focused on her again. I know this is extreme and you may have an opinion about the situation, but for the moment just follow along. She stated that she loved him and he didn't love her. However if she loved him, she would not base her love on the condition that he behaves a certain way toward her, she would simply love him, regardless of his behavior.

If she loved herself she would decide whether or not she would want to continue a relationship with a person that does not treat her the way she wants to be treated. Hurting herself to manipulate attention is neither self love nor love of the other.

Relationships are often tools to find our hearts and our own ability to love ourselves as well as others.

Each challenge is an opportunity to grow and expand. To get back to the above example, the woman's husband is scared. He has caused his wife so much pain that she has hurt herself and he immediately tries to patch things up and showers her with promises and attention. Now I am asking you, is this attention or love that he is displaying? Would you like to be in a relationship that has the guillotine of your partner hurting him- or herself hanging over you?

OK, this may not be anything you can relate to, so how about little issues, like making time for your partner only if they in return also are available when you want them to be. Or the friend that only wants to meet with you, assures you how much you mean to him but you have to always visit him, because his life is so busy he only has a few minutes for you.

Think about your closest relationship issues and examine how much seeking attention is the motivation of your behavior. I have certainly been guilty of manipulating for attention many times.

When I was a kid I became sick in order to get my father's attention. He was a great doctor and healer, so if I was sick and he could help, he would always be there for me, even if under normal circumstances he would have been too busy. At one time I fell in love with a man, who was very busy, but always made time for friends in need. Even though I did not act upon it, the thought of whining loud enough to be heard and get his attention came up several times. Luckily I recognized the attention pattern and realized that I was better off capable and whole within myself than with the attention from a man who did not give it freely.

The other problem with relying on extracted attention is that settling into that structure actually creates a shield from experiencing love. Because it feels similar to real love, some people use pure attention as a "good enough" substitute.

Common belief is that if you never allow yourself to get close to anyone, you will never have to experience the pain of losing love. But like I said before, love is eternal, it is who we are, we cannot lose love.

By cutting yourself off from the experience of love, you are cutting yourself off from the most wonderful part of you; much like the fox who decided that the sweet grapes, which were out of his reach were sour and no good. Instead of waiting for the sweet grapes to fall off the vine and find him, he decides never to experience the real sweetness and delicious taste the grapes held. With an attention shield you wind up restricting yourself and living in a limited love flow setting. It only protects you from experiencing life fully.

Not only is this construct limiting, but it actually winds up being more painful than going through loss or heartbreak. By constantly setting yourself up to receive a poor copy of love, you place yourself in a cycle of lack, the lack of love. This lack reinforces beliefs about the self, about others, about the world, that close your mind and your heart and cause pain. At first it may be a low grade pain, and you may not even notice it. But eventually a discontent will set in, a loneliness from being cut off from the world and from yourself. And this winds up being more hurtful than losing someone or something you have loved.

The following chart will help you quickly check where you stand in your relationships.

Chart 1.1

Attention	Love
Temporary energy that fuels temporary structures in our lives	Pure life force energy that cannot deplete
Often extracted and manipulated	always available and free
*Means you compromise yourself to get what you need	Means you are loved for who you are
Constantly needs to be reestablished and replenished	Eternal and always present

*Note that this is self-compromise and is different from the normal compromise or give and take of healthy relationships.

Next is a good example of someone who got caught in the attention for love cycle.

Kyle's Story

Kyle was 21 and had been going out with his girlfriend for a little over a year. One evening he saw her being intimate with another guy. He was very hurt. His first reaction was to punch a wall breaking a bone in his hand. This temporarily distracted him from his emotional pain. But he didn't stop there. He started telling himself that he was not worth being loved by anyone and years later he had given up on finding a good relationship. The girls he dated were superficial and he was always glad to see them leave. He never gave much of himself and never got much in return.

Kyle punished himself for what someone else had done to him by first breaking a bone and then by not allowing himself to feel love in a relationship again. He had turned against himself in a time of need and, because of that, wound up in a constant state of discontent. At first, not allowing love in again made Kyle feel protected and strong, but eventually it made him feel broken and unworthy of real love.

Ask yourself: would you rather live in constant pain or constant bliss with occasional painful experiences?

Remember, all structure is temporary. So if you choose to place your love needs and wants into any structure, you will eventually experience loss and pain and only a temporary relief of pain. On the other hand if you choose to place your love in the motion and flow of life force, your experience of love is permanent.

I am at a place in life where I still put a lot of my love into structure: my family, my friends, my work, the Pacific Ocean, my artwork and some of my belongings. The amount of pain I experience depends on how much I am attached to experiencing, receiving and giving love through these structures. Because of my attachment pain is inevitable. If I were capable of always experiencing Oneness and the fact that we are all connected within that Oneness, there would be no more pain.

However, I am still of this world, with physical needs and wants. So I expect to experience some emotional pain. Sometimes this pain is so severe that I can't process it by myself and I find help. Other times this pain lingers and stays with me for a while. When it comes up, I remind myself of this: since love is what we are striving to experience and the loss or absence of real loving attention is at the root of emotional pain, the most important thing is to give ourselves the love that we think we lost or are missing and to remind ourselves that we are infinite love.

The following story will give you an example of how loss and grief can be experienced without damaging yourself.

Jason's Story

Jason was married for 37 years to his soul-mate as he described his wife Helen. He always thought he would die before her, but life had other plans. Helen got sick and passed away. Jason was heartbroken and lost. His family, kids and friends came to help him with the funeral arrangements and to get through the first days. He knew that it was her time and he was glad that she went fast without too much suffering.

I spoke with Jason a few weeks after the funeral to see how he was. I knew that by now his family and friends had returned to their lives. He told me that he had joined a bereavement group for support and was busy doing things that were fun for him. He tutored children, traveled on weekends visiting friends and places he liked. He made it a point to get out of the house because it was difficult to be at home without Helen. A few months later, when we spoke again he was no longer traveling as much. He enjoyed being home, feeling Helen's presence in all the things that reminded him of her. Jason said: "I still cry at times, but I am ok."

Jason took care of himself, whether it was getting out of the house or staying at home, surrounding himself with people or being alone. He did exactly what he thought would give him the support he needed to get through this. He was open to flow.

Take another look at how you have dealt with emotional pain in the past.
How have you treated yourself?
Did you take care of yourself with love and compassion?
Did you punish yourself physically?
Did you place restrictions on your life, not allowing yourself to fully experience love and joy following an emotional injury?
Below are some phrases I have heard from clients. Do any of them resonate with you or can you identify your own "truths"?
I will never be happy, because my father abused me.
I can't ever trust someone again, because I was betrayed.
My best friend died when I was 15, ever since then I had no real friends.

Now that you are more aware of how you operate in regard to emotional pain and hopefully made the decision to treat yourself better than ever before let me ask you another question:

Are you ready to experience unlimited love flowing through the motion of your life, even if it means that you will experience the pain of loss of temporary structure?

Chapter 9

Shifting Spiritual Structures

Your spiritual grid encompasses all of your beliefs, your core beliefs as well as your superficial ones. These are the things you hold on to about yourself, the world, God. As mentioned before, these structures are typically rigid and hold within them the concept of being right. Just like the physical and emotional structures, spiritual structures also need to expand and evolve.

As rigid as these beliefs are and as rarely as they shift, the truth is, they are the easiest to shift and heal. In the physical structure, you may wait for a wound to close, a bone to repair; in the emotional structure, you may wait for the pain of loss to dissipate; but in the spiritual structure, all it takes to shift is a simple thought: you are part of everything and everyone in Oneness, a part of the unified field of creation. With this thought alone you have shifted.

Beliefs are nothing more than thoughts we support, focus on and collect evidence for. Every time you form an opinion about something you are moving within a belief structure. Most beliefs separate us from others, because we believe that we are right.

For example if you believe that people who drive white cars are bad drivers, that the color green doesn't look good on your friend, or that your neighbor cuts his lawn too short, you are operating in a specific belief setting. These beliefs, even though they are small carry within them the seed of judgment and separation.

When we realize that we are the cells in the organism of creation, omnipresence, God, all judgment falls away. We consciously become the space, the expanded field experiencing itself within our chosen structures. We come to see that most of the beliefs we hold on to so tightly are illusions of separation. If we imagine the universe as one body this would be akin to our hand saying our foot is wrong because it looks different. When we give up the notion of right or wrong, judgment stops and we can experience Oneness.

While all of the little belief thoughts that fill your mind throughout the day are worth noting, they may not be strong enough to truly hinder your expansion. Therefore I would like to focus on two of the larger types of beliefs people hold.

The beliefs about the self and where one fits into the structures of one's existence and the beliefs about God, religion, or lack of religion, that have to do with how the world operates. The latter includes any belief that has an outside authority pulling the strings, anything and anyone we surrender our authority to, like medical science and doctors.

As you read this chapter, keep in mind that the spiritual shift is unique because instead of waiting for the physical structure to heal (staying in the physical grid) or finding something else in the emotional structure to love (staying in the emotional grid), with the realization of Oneness, you are actually moving from structure to flow of life-force, and in flow all things are possible.

Self-Beliefs And How They Manifest

Do you remember Kyle from the last chapter? His heart was broken and instead of opening himself up to the possibility of love again, he protected himself from this experience. Eventually he *believed* he was not worthy of a real loving relationship. That led to his inability to find a loving partner. Or what about Sam from Chapter 3? He was ill and had gotten so used to people showing their love for him through caretaking that he *believed* that he was only loveable in disease. This caused him to be afraid to get better. Or take Jake from Chapter 5, who believed that everything was a conflict, a challenge to overcome, his self esteem was tied to the belief that he had to battle difficulties to be successful. He was constantly involved in problematic situations where, after battling obstacles, he would come out the victor.

All three men held certain beliefs about themselves that dictated how they fit into their structures. And all three eventually got to the point where the pain of their beliefs outweighed the benefits. With a shift in their perspective, they were able to welcome change and move towards healing.

In these examples, the beliefs about the self were interconnected with the physical and emotional constructs. All constructs are interconnected and shifting one will always shift the others. Kyle was eventually able to shift his emotional grid, Sam was able to heal within his physical structure and Jake was able to put down his sword and allow flow into his life. All three of them had to shift a core belief to effectuate change. In order to shift their belief system, they had to admit that there was the possibility of something existing outside of their beliefs.

83

They also had to be willing to let go of certain fears to find out what that alternative was.

If you answered the reader questions at the end of the last chapter, you may have already come up with a list of self-beliefs that dictate your experiences.

Can you think of any others? If you are stuck, perhaps you can think of situations that you seem to keep experiencing.
Are you repeating any experiences based on a belief?
Is it possible that there is an alternative to the belief that you are holding?

Spiritual Beliefs And How They Guide Us

While our self-beliefs guide our experiences, spiritual beliefs guide our "Experience." Our spiritual belief construct determines how we view life and make decisions about our place in the world and all of creation. If you look at it like a computer, the self-beliefs are like the software and the programs we run, whereas the spiritual beliefs are the hard drive that runs everything.

These spiritual beliefs determine where you live, the kinds of people you associate with, the people you don't associate with. For many people, their spiritual beliefs act as their moral compass and guide their behavior. The most common spiritual belief is, of course, organized religion. This book also centers around a belief: the belief in expansion.

But whether it is religion, atheism, or expansion, ask yourself if it makes sense to you. And before you adopt any belief, please check in with yourself and ask if this rings true or offers possibilities for you.

To shift into Oneness we have to recognize and answer the call to expand our spiritual structure. This call will show up as any issue that challenges being right about something. The degree of difficulty associated with the challenge will depend on the intensity of your attachment to being right, as well as how much of your identity is connected to the issue.

The more attachment the more painful the experience will be. Life will create situations that demand attention and foster expansion. Considering how easy it is to step into Oneness and be whole and free of pain instantly, it is amazing how much pain is still caused by rigid belief structures.

What makes spiritual beliefs easy to shift is the same thing that makes them difficult to shift. Which is that most of our spiritual beliefs are learned and are connected to authority figures: doctors, teachers, pastors, parents, the list goes on. So the moment you believe something that an authority figure says to be true, you are connecting to their belief structure and making it your own. It can be difficult to let go of something a parent or a pastor or even a doctor has told you to be true.

But remember these beliefs are not you, they are just something you are choosing to operate within. Like the other structures, the belief structure is temporary and only the ever-expanding energy that flows through the structure is eternal, is who you are. There is nothing wrong with allowing your life force to flow in the structures of your choice, as a matter of fact that is what living and experiencing life is about. But your essence is going to expand and evolve, therefore I encourage you to look frequently at the structure of your choice to see if it is useful and helps you to expand your flow of life force or if it is choking you?

One of the first examples I like to give to help illustrate the belief structure is the belief in Santa Claus. Most people grow up convinced that there is a Santa Claus who climbs down chimneys and distributes presents once a year. And why? Because their parents told them so. That, and of course Santa Claus is a comforting figure, a benevolent man who rewards good behavior and brings gifts one wants to receive.

Do you remember the day when you figured out that Santa Claus wasn't real? That was a challenge in your belief system. It also meant that the people you trusted and loved had been lying to you. I imagine that, no matter how devastating the blow, you were able to eventually get past it and see St. Nick as the character he was supposed to be. I also imagine that it did not cause you to lose permanent trust in your parents. This is an early life example, where your belief may have been a source of joy for a while. You or others probably did not hurt anyone by holding onto the image of Santa as real. Unfortunately, that is not always the case when it comes to the belief structure.

As with all of our constructs opportunities to shift and expand will show up simply by being alive. First the call will be nothing more then a whisper, maybe an article one reads or a conversation with friends. Since shifting a belief involves giving up and letting go of an existing belief, we rarely listen to the whisper. Instead we often strengthen our existing belief as we proclaim to be right with our opinions. The call will get louder and louder until we listen or our situation becomes so painful that we can't ignore it any longer. The following story illustrates how belief structures can cause unnecessary pain and how they can be resolved.

Nancy's Story

Nancy and her brother grew up in a home with a strong religious structure. In college, she fell in love with a man from a different religious background. Her father threatened to end all contact with her if she were to marry outside of their religion. Even though Nancy loved her father very much, she loved Mark even more and left home forever.

At her wedding, which was supposed to be the happiest time of her life, her brother was the only relative in attendance.

Her mother was no longer alive and her father had cut off ties completely.

In this example, Nancy's father acted contrary to the people he loved based on a strong set of beliefs. He chose not to follow one of his first calls to shift by accepting his daughter's choice and attending her wedding, regardless of his beliefs.

The end of Nancy's story is bittersweet. After her wedding, her father attached himself and all of his hopes onto Nancy's brother. But the brother also fell in love with someone from a different religion. Not knowing how to tell his father, he became depressed, started drinking and ultimately died in an accident. The father was devastated and lonely. In his grief and after years of misery and pain, the father contacted Nancy again. He was finally able to see that he and his structures were the cause of all this pain. He was able to expand and let Nancy's husband and children be part of his life. He was lucky that she let him come back into her life and be a grandfather to her children. Even though many painful years passed before the shift happened, when he shifted it happened instantaneously.

I do not mean to imply you ever have to give up what is right for you at any given time but I am asking you to examine your beliefs, question their validity for you, and not make others adhere to your beliefs. Your structures are for you, they will never fit someone else, just like your body is yours and not someone else's. Most belief systems stem from authority figures. This means that someone has decided that their belief structure is good for you, and maybe it is. In any case don't just buy into it without checking how it works for you. Ask yourself how does this structure fit? And recognize when it is time for a new one. Know that you are the one living your life and could be paying a price for the structure.

The next story is another example how belief constructs can be difficult to change, but the examination and reward of questioning and changing if needed can lead to experiencing love and bliss not thought possible before.

Daniel's Story

Daniel is homosexual. He grew up in a family and community that believed that homosexuals can't get into heaven, that they were doomed and sick and possessed by evil. His family loved him dearly and wanted the best for him, but they suffered at the thought that their son would not be granted eternal life due to his sexual preference. Daniel suffered because he was an outcast of his family and community, and was constantly plagued by guilt over his desires and thoughts.

Daniel's mother and surrounding community did not hate him. In fact, they loved and cared about him so much that they were afraid he would suffer greatly if he didn't change to fit into their construct. In their rigid belief, they knew that they were right. For Daniel it meant that he was doomed no matter what he chose to do. He could deny who he was to remain inside of this structure, in which case the God of that belief would know his real thoughts anyway. Or he could stand behind himself and continue to be ostracized from the community and eventually denied possible entry into heaven.

Daniel chose a third option, to question the structure he had been given and step out of it or expand it to be able to include him. He left home and eventually found a community of friends who helped him cope with his situation. He was able to expand his belief structure and now no longer believes that he is doomed and rejected by God for being homosexual. After he felt secure with who he was he started to communicate with his mother again slowly convincing her to open and expand her beliefs, so she too could feel better about having a child like him. In this situation, there was an opportunity for Daniel to expand and he brought that opportunity to his mother and to his community.

When confronted with an opportunity to question a belief structure, you have to do it from within and without. From within meaning what does your inner compass say? Does this feel right? And from without, by analyzing the structure and by looking around at evidence of an alternative. So in Daniel's case, he asked how could God create something faulty that he would deny entry to his kingdom? Is God not almighty after all? Are all homosexual people plagued by the same problem or are others dealing differently with their sexual preference? Are there homosexual people who are living happy, accepted lives? Are there other homosexual people who believe in God? He allowed himself to challenge the belief and then found evidence to support his expansion.

Daniel's and Nancy's stories deal with the religious structure and although their stories may not directly reflect your structures, I hope they inspire you to look into your own belief systems to see if your construct is working for you or if it is time to expand. I know many people who have similar experiences as Daniel and Nancy in regard to their race, nationality, education, or social status. The belief to stick to one's own kind is still very prevalent in society today. But that only limits our experiences, rather than opens us up to the possibilities of a full existence.

I was fortunate to have grown up in a household with a fairly open belief system. Loving thy neighbor was more important in my home than any doctrine ostracizing other people. Any belief that is not inclusive of the universe as a whole and includes all of humanity does not make sense to me. This is something I try to instill in my kids as well.

One time my 8-year old son came home after watching a movie with friends about God who allowed Satan to take all non-believers with him to hell while all believers went to heaven. Now, mind you, I had no idea he was watching something like that but even so, it barely affected him. He walked in the door and said: "I can't believe in any God who would do something like that, but Tim does and that's ok, got to go play", and out he ran again.

My daughter is much more quiet about her beliefs. They are personal to her and she doesn't usually want to discuss them. But if she is present during a discussion on beliefs, she will point out that the outsider in the discussion has a point that can be just as right. I guess they call that playing Devil's advocate and with that part of her she keeps me on my toes. If I make a statement judging the behavior or opinion of another, she'll say: "Who made you the boss of everyone, mom?" Busted! Sometimes it takes me a moment to get over myself but in the end we laugh about it.

Even though I tend to be inclusive in my beliefs, I too have moments of judgment and separation. Years ago a dear friend of mine decided to go through a male to female transgender process. When she first told me about it, my belief that we are here in our body to experience what life deals us was challenged. Changing nature was not what I believed in. As I pondered the question for myself I mentioned it to my teenage son, as we were driving home from school. He told me he had to think how he felt about it. After a few moments he told me that if it made our friend feel better it was totally ok.

My son was much faster at expanding than I was. It took him 3 minutes and me about an hour. Had I not been able to expand my belief I would have lost one of my best friends and limited my life experience. And really, how could I know what is right for him better than he knows himself. So while I try to teach my kids about inclusion, it is more often that they teach me.

Beliefs About Healing

Religious beliefs are not the only place where spiritual structure manifests. Health and wellness beliefs can also work along similar lines. Many people place their faith in science or healing modalities. For many, doctors or healers hold the key to the body, often knowing more than the person living in that body. But the truth is they are not your body, nor are they aware of what your body is capable of. They are experts in a field and the information they provide may be of use to you. But there is the possibility that it may not be helpful. Doctors operate from their beliefs and often will state their findings as rigid facts for which they have collected ample evidence.

If you blindly step into a doctor's belief system, you are limited to the possibilities within that system. Often you will start to look for evidence within your own body to prove that this new belief system is correct. Your general direction and focus now points toward proving the belief system rather than to being open to a miracle or alternative. Your innate power to connect to the universal energy has been exchanged for a limited structure. I urge you to keep in mind that there is no one out there who knows your body better than you do.

When confronted with a medical issue, check in with yourself, harmonize your decisions about moving forward and move into the direction of your choice. Your doctor or healer may be spot on with what they are recommending and deep down you know if that is the case.

Ann's Story

Ann discovered that she had shingles. This happened while on a trip with friends in South America. The small town doctor had no access to the then newer anti viral drugs to help her. He suggested she go to see the old lady healer in the next town.

He explained to her that shingles was a psychic disease and was easy to heal. Based on that, Ann pictured an old witch, who would make her drink poisonous potions that might even kill her. She opted not to go and see if the woman could help. In her belief construct, healers were just quacks with nothing to offer. She tried to continue her trip but felt so bad that she returned home early.

When I met her a few years later she laughed about herself as she told the story. She added that after the shingles wouldn't go away for months a friend took her to a healer in the States who was able to help her. She said, "I wish I could have been more open. I missed out on a great trip with my friends and experienced pain for many weeks."

Ann's story clearly demonstrates how her rigid belief in a certain kind of medicine kept her from having a wonderful trip with friends. She was not able to expand her structure until she had been sick and in pain for a long time. Her shingles only affected her experience.

But what about someone who is offered a medical treatment that is useful, who decides to suffer through pain rather than taking a medical approach, or a parent that won't bring their child to a certain kind of doctor? Or people who don't believe in administering medication? Again, there is no right or wrong here, just choices and consequences of our choices.

Take a look at where you are with your belief structures about health.
How are they affecting yourself or others around you?

There is so much we don't know and sometimes the uncertainty drives us to hold onto certain beliefs for stability. But remember, that stability is an illusion guided by fear. Something born out of fear cannot support you in Oneness or open you up to the flow of life's possibilities. I would like you to consider that there is no right or wrong, just colorful differ-

92

ences like wildflowers on a beautiful summer meadow. Pick the flowers that are right for you. If you are unsure, take a look at it and be open to putting it down and picking a different flower.

Become aware of your opinions. Keep a notepad and every time you have an opinion, write it down. At the end of the day, go through your list.
What triggered that opinion?
Is the opinion causing you to separate from anyone you love?
Could that opinion be connected to a whisper of change?
Is there room in any of your opinions for an alternative?

If you are adamant or stubborn about there not being an alternative to something, I urge you to look at that one again.

PART IV

The Tool Chest

There are three easy to use tools for healing and shifting just about anything within your Universe. First we will explore forgiveness to heal our wounds as well as the structures that keep us confined because of our wounds. Second we will set course in the direction of our dreams through gratitude and third we will explore our true genetic possibilities.

Chapter 10

Forgive, Let Go And Heal Yourself, Your Surroundings And The Universe

Everything in the Universe is connected, if one person heals him- or herself, everything in the Universe will be affected by it. Every time you heal yourself you open the door for others to heal as well. Healing yourself is doing community service.

In the past chapters we have looked at what happens when structure has outgrown its usefulness. Now let's explore how to let go of what no longer serves us, so we can heal, expand and move forward. The best and easiest way to let go of anything is to forgive and release. Through forgiving and letting go of the issues connected to a specific construct, everything that once held you in the confinement of that construct is released.

As long as you see yourself as a victim of any kind of event or structure in your life, you are connected and held in place by it. Holding on to your role of victim is, in effect, holding onto a construct that is no longer benefitting you. The reality is that all events that seem to make you a victim of circumstance are nothing more than a call to expand, a necessary universal nudge from an event or person, who, on some level, wants the best for you. A person who wants you to grow and find your new expanded self.

Let's go back to the image of the spider's web from earlier. Remember I mentioned that we create a web to operate within, to serve as our infrastructure. And simultaneously, we represent the fly caught in our own web. Following this image, everything you hold onto is a thread catching you in your own web. Every judgment you hold also holds you.

The best teachers in life are those who push us the furthest, those who aggravate us the most and even those who hurt us. They are the ones who force us to leave our comfort zones and expand. A comfort zone is just that, comfortable, it is where we want to be. It is usually a place we are familiar with, where we know what is happening, that the rent or mortgage is going to be paid, the food is on the table, and that there are no unpleasant surprises. But what happens to muscles when they sit on the comfortable couch day after day? They atrophy, and that also happens to our emotional, mental and spiritual muscles; when they are not challenged they also atrophy.

For our bodies we go to the gym, and push ourselves through sore muscles to new capabilities. Sometimes we hire trainers who tell us to go on when we really want to give up, get into a hot shower and relax. Lucky for us, the trainers of life are free, we don't need to go out and hire one, the universe has an ample supply for us free of charge, to push and help us excel.

These coaches come in many different forms, relationship partners, children, coworkers, parents, people that we interact with in close proximity as well as politicians, dictators, or others who affect our lives from a distance and just about any annoying person. These people make us look outside of our comfort box. They scratch on the box and interfere with what we have found to be our zone.

At first this person is an intruder and we try to patch up the scratches and protect against further intrusion, but eventually our box will break. Oftentimes, even though the box is broken and we seem to have moved on, we are still schlepping the debris of the box, the hurt, the fear, the anger or resentment of having the box fall apart in the first place. The only way to free ourselves from this unnecessary burden is to forgive the intruder, who allowed us to see that there is a freer much more expanded place outside the box.

Let's compare it to the process of being born. Birth, I imagine, is scary for a fetus. After surviving the passage down the birth canal in total darkness the baby enters a new space. First the baby needs to detach from the previous home, the warm comfortable environment that has been safe and nourishing for so long. Then the umbilical cord needs to be cut in order for the baby to live life.

Everything that fetus has known and relied on is cut away in an instant as a new expanded world appears. Neither the mother, nor the midwife, the doctor or whoever aids in the delivery of the baby is viewed negatively even though they cut the link to the only thing that baby has ever known. On the contrary, they are celebrated, as is this moment of new life.

Today in delivery rooms the father is often asked to cut the cord. Imagine how a baby might feel about that. After your mother expels you from your universe, the second most important person to you finishes the job. He could be viewed as a "bad guy" for taking the last of the known environment away from the baby. But of course we know he is not the bad guy, but a loving caring father, willing to be present for this important step in the life of his baby, giving the last and very loving cut to propel his child into life.

Our lives keep moving in pretty much the same way, we constantly outgrow the environments and constructs we know and our very best supporters will help us cut the cords and rejoice in the maybe painful, maybe scary, and definitely exciting new developments. So who are our best teachers and our strongest supporters? They are not always the most obvious players or the most outwardly loving. Most people are familiar with the story of Jesus, so let's take a look at that story for a moment and explore the different people who played pivotal roles in his being able to spread his message.

Imagine that one of Jesus' plans is to show and teach people that death is not the end, that life or existence goes on afterwards. He wants to demonstrate resurrection from death and while he is planning an event to illustrate this, he realizes that he actually has to go through death himself. Because he wants a large amount of people to witness this event he has to create a grand performance. Getting ready to set up the plan, the acting persons need to be cast in their roles. There are the roles for Mother Mary and Joseph and other supports.

Everyone is going to audition for those roles, and those that earn them are souls that are highly evolved and ultimately fondly remembered. Now Jesus also needs to cast the other roles, the executioners who nail him to the cross, Judas who betrays him, the angry mob that demands his crucifixion, etc. I don't think I would like to play any of those parts, would you? But without anyone taking on those roles, the grand event would not have happened. The awareness of the existence of life after death, the importance of letting go by forgiving your enemies even if they nail you to the cross, the possibility of resurrection and many more amazing insights would not have been revealed to so many people.

Now think about it, wouldn't it take strong supporters of Jesus to do something like that for him? I think it would and then those beings will eventually be given a chance to evolve through learning, self-forgiving and expansion etc. There are

100

opportunities for everyone to grow and expand. We have all played different characters at different times and we keep expanding and evolving with new challenges all the time.

Is there anyone in your life that has ever told you, you couldn't do something or who said profoundly hurtful things to you? An ex-spouse, a mean teacher, a parent?
What did you do with that information?
Did you pull back and stop exploring life or did you counteract those comments to become something greater?
Were you able to move past the negative, see how every event in your life has lead up to this glorious moment of being alive, of being you, the flow of love energy?
Or do you still struggle with those threads in your web? If so, keep reading for some tools that will help you let go of what is holding you in place.

Letting Go

How do we let go? There are many tools available to forgive and let go. One of my favorites stems from my understanding of Ho'opono'ono, a Hawaiian healing method. There are many books and classes on Ho'opono'ono for those of you who would like to delve deeper into it. Here is my simplified 4 step version, which has helped me let go of just about anything that is no longer useful. After the 4 steps below, I will take you through a couple of practical applications so you can see specifically how they work.

Step 1: Take Responsibility

Everything I experience, see, read, hear about is my creation and my responsibility. I am the creator of my life and therefore if something/someone is in my life it, he or she has become my responsibility. All things are there because they

101

correspond to something within me that needs healing or expansion. It often takes over the top, cruel or annoying behavior to get my attention.

At the moment when I am confronted with something or someone that hits a nerve, I need to take responsibility by acknowledging that I have invited this into my life. If it's a person, in some respects, I have created this being in my life and have made them so completely over the top, so that they get my attention. This means that this person had to go through certain life experiences and possibly suffer to become the being, this very irritating being, who has gotten under my skin. I acknowledge that I myself have put that person through all those experiences. The moment that I understand this I am humbled. In the depth of this humble feeling I say to myself and to the spirit of whomever I am acknowledging:

I take responsibility for creating you this way... so that I can heal myself.

Step 2: Apology

As I realize what I have created and how much I have put my creations through to bring about my own healing I now ask for forgiveness:

Please forgive me, for all I have put you through so I can have this awareness and healing experience.
I apologize from the depth of my being, from the core of my heart.

Step 3: Gratitude

I am so thankful that you have gone through so much just for me. I am thankful that you did such an amazing job:

I am grateful for your love for me and with humble gratitude I thank you from my deepest core.

Step 4: Love

Now, after I have taken responsibility, have apologized and ask for forgiveness and have thanked everyone for their part in my expansion, I am ready to move forward. I have learned what I needed to learn from the event and freed myself from having to repeat the same issue over and over. I am ready to let go and move on. I do this by releasing the issue and all involved from the structures of the event back into life force energy. I do this by saying the following to everyone involved:

I love you.

And while I say these words to the Universe I now release everyone connected to me through this issue from this moment all the way back to the beginning of creation. I release and let love wash away all the signs of this issue.

This simple method, *I apologize, please forgive me, thank you, I love you,* creates miracles whenever it is implemented. To get a better understanding of it I included Cameron's story, which deals with relationship challenges, and Leanne's story of abuse and how they used the 4 steps to heal their lives.

Cameron's Story

Cameron was divorced with three teenage kids. He was in a management job that he hated but it supported him and his kids while also covering the alimony payments to his ex wife. He wanted to be a teacher, something he felt a calling for since he was a little boy. His parents thought he could do better and that he would make more money if he got an MBA. While at the University, he met his girlfriend and she accidentally became pregnant. His father helped support them while Cameron finished school with the condition that they get married.

After graduating, his father helped him get his first job. He thought of himself as ungrateful for all his father had done for him and tried not to think about how much he disliked his life. He did love his daughter and his wife. Soon they had two more children. Melanie, his wife had dropped out of school to raise the children. As the years went on Cameron became more and more grumpy when he was home, because his days were filled with activities he did not enjoy. Melanie was equally frustrated because she had not finished school and had given up her dreams to support Cameron.

The marriage fell apart and the divorce was packed with each other's frustrations. Cameron had quit his job and Melanie had taken that as a sign that he had no interest in supporting his children. In her anger she told the children that if their dad was not so selfish, they could have the things they needed and wanted.

This is when I met Cameron. He sat in my office telling me how everyone in his life wanted him to be miserable, how his children didn't like him and that he was depressed and didn't know what to do. Furthermore, his searches for business jobs had come up empty.

I asked him about his dream of being a teacher, and he batted away the notion because as a teacher he wouldn't earn enough money to pay for child support and alimony and he certainly wouldn't be able to support himself. I pointed out to him that he was not able to do this on unemployment either. After a short time he realized that he needed to shift and let go in order to move to a place of peace and joy. We started the 4 step process with his ex wife as the subject of our focus.

In the first step he realized that he had gotten a second chance to move in the direction of his dreams because she had forced him to look at his life and set him free with the divorce. He took a look back in time at her life up to that point. She had gotten pregnant very young, given up her dream of a career and degree to support him. She had sacrificed her youth, her youthful body, her dream of a happy marriage and many more little things, so that she could get him to the point where he was now; the point of reevaluating his life and dreams and possibilities.

When he realized this he started to cry and said: "she did so much for me, I never realized it before." With the words described in Step 1 he took responsibility and acknowledged her amazing role in his life: *I take responsibility for creating you, this way... so that I can heal myself.*

The next three steps followed naturally, he imagined her in front of him and apologized for everything he had put her through, asking her to forgive him: *I apologize for all the hardship I have put you through, please forgive me.*

Still in tears he told the image of her how grateful he was for everything: *thank you* and with a heartfelt: *I love you,* he released her image back to the Universe.

He returned to his hometown and immediately looked for any kind of work. He landed another business job but he didn't mind doing this kind of work since his ex-wife had done so much for him. The next time he picked up his kids, he spent some time talking to her and asking her what she wanted to do with her life. He wanted to know how he could support her and her dreams by being more actively involved with the kids.

Their relationship became amicable and a year later I heard from Cameron, he was babysitting his ex wife's new son. She had remarried a man who was much better suited for her according to Cameron. His kids adjusted well to the situation because everyone involved was treated respectfully. Cameron eventually went back to school to get his teaching credentials and to follow his heart.

Leanne's Story

Leanne grew up in an abusive household. Her father and later her foster father abused her physically and sexually. When she went to her mother for help, her mother blamed her for ruining her marriage and the family and gave her to a foster family. Leanne was getting thinner and thinner.

One of her school teachers noticed Leanne was having a tough time and befriended the girl. Leanne did not talk about her situation and shut down at any personal questions. The teacher was patient and talked only about school related issues, and invited her to school related trips to the museum and book signings. The teacher talked about herself and difficult situations in her own life until Leanne opened up a little at a time. Finally she took Leanne to support groups and then to a therapist.

By that time Leanne had turned 18 and was legally on her own. Her father, who wanted the story of his actions hidden, would send her care packages and money to show how much he cared for her, and to keep her from moving forward. Over the next few years Leanne learned to like herself and stand up for herself with the help of therapists, counselors and friends.

She continued to study and became a dental assistant. One day she met a man she really liked. Over a long dating period they got closer. Leanne did not see herself as capable of intimacy and so she discouraged any relationship efforts her suitor made. But he was not easily discouraged and together they worked on healing.

When I met Leanne she was well on her way to recovery, but she still had a lot of hate for her father that came up any time she thought about intimacy. This, of course, did not benefit her relationship. Her boyfriend was on the brink of giving up and moving on. She loved him but could not get over her baggage.

I took her love for her boyfriend as an entry point. I mentioned to her how miraculous it was that they had met. We focused on all the wonderful things that had appeared in her life, her teacher and now good friend, the wonderful counselors and therapists, her friends from the various support groups. I pointed out that many people from those same support groups had been helped and encouraged by her to step forward in their lives.

She began to see herself with purpose and awe. What had actually helped her get there, what had pushed her through so much experience and learning? We ultimately established that her father and foster father had helped her get there. They had given her experiences that had led to this amazing strong person she now was.

Now please understand I am not condoning abuse and misery in any way. These events had already happened just as any unpleasant events from your past. Events are always going to happen, and some of them are going to be unpleasant or even bad. The goal of the first step is to see yourself as a creator rather than as a victim, so that you can move forward in your life instead of staying within the abusive structure, leading your life from the role of an abuse victim.

I asked Leanne to follow along in a story, a life story, her story. I asked her to imagine herself as the creator of her life, to see herself as the director and producer, who had hired all the actors, as well as directed the performances. Leanne was asked to focus on her father first, who had been the most abusive person in her life from early on. In order to be such an abusive person her father had to live through a number of challenges and hardships. He had to learn how to be abusive and cruel. I asked Leanne to see the hardship he had to endure in order to perform such an abusive father role in her play. I asked her to see the incredible sacrifices he had made to become the person he was for his role in her life.

First she thought this was a little far fetched but she followed along and while focusing on her father's role, she realized what he had gone through to become the person he played in her story. She thought about it for a while and took responsibility for her story.

She was humbled when thinking about the difficult life her father had had in order to become who he was in her story. And just for this moment she felt sorry to have put him through all this hardship in her story, her script. Feeling hum-

107

bled she apologized to the spirit of her father and asked him to forgive her, as described in step two. This was followed by tears and a great sense of gratitude in step three, and she released the whole story into the essence of love with a heartfelt: *I love you*.

Leanne never saw her father again, she had broken all contact with him long before and he had died a few years prior to our work together. After the forgiving work on her father, she continued with her foster father, her mother and all the other people involved. She felt so much better that she couldn't wait to release all the people from her past. She now saw all the events as leading up to a wonderful story of love and trust and passion. She got married to her boyfriend and after more than 10 years of marriage they are still like newly weds.

The four step process of forgiving and letting go can be done anytime with anyone. When going through it, there is no need for the other person to be involved, present or even alive. The process is *not* about the other person. It is about healing the self. What is important is that we release the past and enjoy the present. If I were to claim that I can never be happy because someone else did something to me, I will have created an unhappy structure, in which I would live my life, punishing only myself, not anyone else. Leanne's father was long dead therefore his life was no longer affected by the abuse. She was the one carrying on the suffering and allowing it to affect her life.

The Universe always answers the requests and rearranges itself to accommodate the constructs we have chosen. Situations will appear in line with the evidence needed to support the individual's view of life. More and more things will happen that support the construct until the restrictive structure becomes unbearable. Finally it will break down to allow expansion into increased flow of love energy.

Forgiveness is the easiest most painless road to travel.

Take a look at the four steps and see the many areas in your life where you can apply the process and watch how easy it is to leave the shackles, balls and chains behind.

Who are the people in your life that you consider your ball and chain?

Who or what memory stops you from being the best you can be?

For example, is there something someone did or said in your past that is a source of shame or embarrassment to this day?

Who do you use as an excuse to be less than you want to be?

Give it a try, see if you can forgive and change some of the areas in your life. Forgiving is the your gift to yourself.

Chapter 11

Gratitude

Keeping your Focus in the right Direction

Forgiveness is the most important tool to move into health and well-being, but it focuses on events of the past. Forgiveness should be implemented anytime an issue comes up that reminds you of the past, or every time you hold or utter a judgment about any person or event. But right after the forgiving process is complete, you are done looking behind you. It is now time for your focus to shift back to your future goals and the direction you would like to move in. This shift is easiest achieved through gratitude.

Let's briefly think about driving a car again. You start with an idea of where you want to go. If your car is too heavily loaded with baggage and hooked-on trailers full of stuff, it will hardly move even with a full tank of gas and the pedal to the metal. In life, that baggage can be fear, pain, self-loathing, anything that holds you back. In addition you may have filled your car's tank with a poor substitute for gas.

Remember, in chapter 8, we talked about temporary energy solutions like receiving attention. Or some people gravitate towards addictive substances to fuel themselves. Addictive substances are extremely short term solutions and most of them will also damage your structure. With all that baggage and inferior gas, chances are you're not going very far. Because your car is not moving forward you keep looking in the review mirror to see what is holding you back. Your focus is not on your desired destination, it is on your baggage. To make matters more intense, your energy will move in the direction of your focus. So even if your car starts to move forward, while your focus is fixed on what is behind you, you will eventually crash your car and add another pain and failure to your experience and baggage.

In order to move forward, forgiving and letting go has to be either like a quick look over your shoulder at your blind spot, or, if you feel you need time to spend on the process, park your car at a rest stop, deal with the forgiveness at hand, dispose of the baggage effectively and completely, and then continue your trip. Once back on the road, the best way to keep your focus ahead and on your destination is through gratitude.

Everything in life is energy, information and moving particles. The future does not exist until it is present, therefore anything can happen. When you are grateful for achieving a goal, you energize the picture of reality that holds the achievement of that goal. You activate energies in the Universe to support you, to bring the particles together that result in your goal. Keep in mind that sometimes the universe has a better knowledge of what would be a good goal or result for you. This means you will receive what you need rather than what you think you want. Or maybe halfway to your goal you decide to change directions. Either way you can't go anywhere unless you are moving. You may or may not reach the goal the way you envision it but you will head in the general direction of your desires, which will result in events that are congruent with your objective.

A Gratitude Tool

I keep a gratitude journal, a little notebook on my bedside table. Almost every morning, I write at least one page of the things I am grateful for, some that have already occurred, some are things in my present life and some have not yet occurred but are events that I desire or goals I want to attain. For example, I am grateful for my kids, I am grateful to have all my needs met, I am grateful for my car, I am grateful for my clients, I am grateful for my health, I am grateful for my friends etc., those are things that I have in my life at the moment I write this and for which I feel gratitude.

Recently I sprained my ankle, so I wrote in my journal: I am grateful for my strong and perfect ankle, as if it were all healed. The universe responds to energy. By feeling grateful for my strong and healed ankle I am radiating the energy of the finished healing process and the universe responds by getting me there. Another example is writing this book. I wrote that I am grateful for the finished book, I am grateful for the inspiration and so on.

When I started this book I had no idea about how to write, publish and find an editor to work with. I wrote in my gratitude journal that I am grateful for all the support and help I am getting in putting this book together. In the beginning, I was often tempted to give up, but whenever those thoughts came up a friend or event would come along and disperse the discouragement. During one of my down moments, I tagged along with a friend to her Toastmaster group.

On that day the featured speaker spoke on book publishing made easy. A few weeks later I was searching for an editor online. I was lost and confused about how to select the right person when I remembered someone I had met briefly months earlier. I asked her advice on how to select the right editor, never even considering that she would take on my book. As our emails progressed, we decided to work together and Molly turned out to be the perfect editor for me.

Now I write that I am grateful to have an amazing editor, and before I wrote that I am grateful to have an amazing editor. The entries regarding the editor or the book in my gratitude journal have not changed. Even in moments of intense pain I write that I am grateful that my body feels good etc. Gratitude will help you keep your direction and focus the energies on the manifestation of the desired goal.

If you have involved other people in your ability to reach your goal you will be tied to their ability to move in your direction. Therefore it is best to phrase goals in terms of how you want to feel or where you want to be and not with whom. For example if you want to have a relationship with a specific person, personal or business, your success is dependent on that person's vision and life. If you just involve yourself in the vision and goal you are open for the right players to show up, you allow the universe to come up with possibilities that exceed your vision.

There is no right or wrong way of keeping a gratitude journal. It's very easy. I mix it up and write what comes to mind, not separating future goals from present or past events. But I want all of it to carry the same weight and energy. Since the feeling is more solid with the things and events that are already tangible in my life, I write down more of them. This enhances the intensity, which carries over to the things I desire.

In order to get into the feeling of gratitude you have to be at the point of having achieved the goal already. If you are grateful for wanting or desiring something or a goal and you write it down as: I am grateful for desiring the future goal, you will reinforce the energy of wanting, desiring and not having.

114

For example I am grateful that the new job is coming into my life puts out the energy of a new job on the way, instead of working in a new job. It is best to write in end result pictures. This is why it is very important to write about the things you already have and are grateful for. If you get stuck coming up with a place to start, just think that the fact that you are able to read this book offers a large amount of things to be grateful for.

Write a page of all the things you are grateful for starting with your heartbeat and breath, your life, this day...
I am grateful for.................

Chapter 12

Activating The Creative Gene

Creativity is everyone's inherited genetic feature. Forgiveness and gratitude are tools to use with issues in your daily life as they show up moment to moment. Forgiveness will free you from a past offense so you can refocus on the moment. Gratitude will set the energy for the moment to be joyful and will make you aware of the countless blessings everywhere.

The third tool I am offering you will help you connect to your genetic heritage, the space of Oneness and infinite possibility. In this space of Oneness, we are pregnant with creativity and constantly giving birth to new ideas, thoughts and possibilities. If you study history, you will notice that everything tends to repeat itself in different settings. Sometimes one country is in power and later another. But overall, it's the same game over and over.

As humans we tend to repeat what we know and expect different results. But in science we know that if we mix the same ingredients or subject the same substances to the same elements we get the same result. The key to creating something new is to do something new or use new ingredients. But most of all, you have to be open to experiencing a result that you have never had before.

Take a moment to look at the fact that you expect pretty specific results with almost all actions you do. For example if you go to work you expect certain things to happen there. If you go out on a date with someone you expect to have either a good, neutral, or bad experience. Whatever you do, you usually have a thought about the result in terms of its being something you have experienced before or at least experienced in your mind. With this kind of presupposition, you become closed off from frequencies that may surpass anything you've encountered or imagined. In the process, your creativity and experience become limited. Holding onto a projected future can act like a security blanket for most of us, shielding us from the fear of potential loss. It takes faith and guts to allow your spirit to guide you into a new experience.

But the moment you connect in Oneness to everything there is, all fear vanishes. You become aware of being a part of all there is, a drop in the pool of Oneness, a Oneness that has existed before you, after you and right now. And in this space there is no loss, no fear. Oneness is our genetic heritage. The space we all come from and return to. So why not enter into the great expanse, it is there for you.

To experience Oneness we have to step out of the structures that house us. Our genetic features, race and DNA are all part of a construct and can be particularly challenging to let go of. Because most of you are familiar with the story of Christmas I chose the following example to illustrate the point. In the birth story of Jesus we are offered a release from the confines of physical genetics. The story tells us that we are not bound to the diseases and problems of our parents and ancestors.

118

Our parents are simply vehicles into the human body, into this life. I like to view parents as the limousine that picks you up at the airport and delivers you to the doorstep of your life. The life you have to live yourself. Let's apply this to the story of Jesus. Mary and Joseph were his vehicles into this world. Mary was a virgin, meaning her genetics were not involved in the creation of this new person. Joseph also did not add his genetics to the formation of the fetus, since the seed came directly from God. They were simply surrogates.

Interestingly enough, the Bible never describes Jesus as looking different from people in the general geographic area. I am certain if he would have looked Asian, Northern European, African or outer worldly it would have been mentioned. His body was composed to fit into his surroundings even though he was not connected to the genetics of his earthly parents.

It doesn't matter much if you believe the story to be real or not, what matters is that the story illustrates a different option, the option to see the omnipresent God space, with its infinite and eternal creative powers and possibilities as your genetic heritage and gift, the opportunity to be in this world but not of it.

I'd like to invite you on a journey to connect your genetics to the infinite life-force energy.
What if you could see yourself as genetically free from the limits of our ancestors?

Meditation

Below is a meditation I offer to help you enter into this space of infinite Oneness. When you read it, make sure to pause where indicated by three dashes --- to allow yourself time to deeply follow along. You can also ask someone else to guide you through it or record it for yourself so that you can just listen. As with all guided meditation, make sure to only do this when you can become deeply relaxed. Do not listen to it while driving or operating any kind of machinery or while being engaged in any activity that requires your attention.

Find a place where you are comfortable and undisturbed.

Allow yourself to relax, close your eyes and focus your attention on your heart center. Just observe, don't change anything. Observe and see how your heart center feels at this moment. Allow whatever is going on in your heart center to continue, just accept and observe as you breathe ---

Imagine a golden light in the center of your heart. Move toward the light. As you get closer you notice that the point of light is located on a golden line. This golden line is your lifeline and the point of golden light is the present moment on your lifeline ---

Imagine your lifeline like a laser light.

Without thinking about any specific events in your life just follow the golden line back through your life. If you notice that there are places where the light is diminished in any form simply ask it to self-repair. Maybe you encounter places with dust that diffuse the light or a tightness that only allows a small amount of light to go through, or a bend in the line, allow it to self repair ---

Any weakening of light force may be connected to events in your life but you don't need to know what they are, just stay with the golden laser light and allow it to self repair. Go all the way back to the moment of your conception. Observe the bright golden light in the first cell of your body ---

Now imagine three lines of light connected to your first cell. One line is your genetic evolutionary line, your parents and ancestors.

Take that line and separate it from your cell, this line holds information for the set design of your life, your ethnic background and body suit for your experiences here on earth. Allow that light line to simply move to the background design and breathe ---

Your stage of life is taken care of and needs no further attention at this time, allow all the influences carried in this genetic, evolutionary line to carry out their roles in the stage design ---

Now focus on the next line of light coming to your first cell. This is your karmic line, your soul experiences, your past lives, your previous interactions, actions and effects. This line also holds information for the play of your life. It holds the script for some of the scenes and acts in your play. I'd like you to also separate it from your cell now. Allow it to gently move to the theater of life experiences. This karmic line will join the genetic line for the play. Allow the karmic light line to simply move to the background stage and breathe ---

You have one line left, a bright and golden light line. Follow this line back further and further, past the creation of earth, our solar system, the Universe, until you reach eternity, pulsating God energy, there is nothing else just energy and you are part of this pulsating God energy ---

This energy has the strong desire to experience itself to know what it feels like. Observe as the desire is becoming stronger and stronger. The desire is becoming so strong that it can't be contained anymore. Imagine the birth of a golden grid forming from the pulsating energy, like channels of energy shooting into empty space ---

As this grid gets larger and larger, notice that there are smaller sub-grids forming. These sub-grids and structures are filling in, they are becoming stars and planets. Observe how the energy is cre-

ating the universe. You are still in the pulsating energy desiring experience, just observe ---

Now imagine traveling through one of those grid lines. Just like electricity through wires. You are travelling towards your first cell in this body, past all the amazing wonders of creation ---

Now you are reaching your first cell. Here you are pulsating God energy in a cell, dividing and multiplying, forming the grid for your body---

Watch as your body emerges---

Allow yourself to travel on this golden lifeline all the way to the present moment. Again, if you encounter anything or any events that appear to diminish the light just ask it to self-repair. You don't need to know what it is, let go and allow it to self-repair ---

Now as you arrive in the present take a moment to observe how you feel ---

Observe your heart center. Just observe ---

Now follow the light line in the other direction, into the future. Focus only on the golden light line. If you encounter any events or anything at all that appears to diminish the light just ask it to self-repair and observe how the light line is getting stronger, more vibrant and brighter ---

Follow the light all the way to infinity. Follow it back to the pulsating God energy where everything comes together again, the place where infinity and eternity meet. You have returned to the place of origin. Where you are part of the pulsating God energy of Oneness ---

Look out at your grid line. It is like a breath, your exhale into creation and inhale back to Oneness ---

Just experience the breath of creation with every inhale and exhale ---

Now come back to your heart center in the present moment. Take all this information and put it in your heart center. You are all of creation. Just like a drop of ocean is all of the ocean.
You are God energy experiencing itself in a body. Everything you encounter is nothing more than an experience.
Breathe ---

Feel the connection in your lifeline ---

Breathe ---

Slowly return to the present moment and open your eyes.

It is good to drink a glass of water after the meditation. As you move through the rest of this day, and in the future, allow yourself to see life from a perspective of yourself as the creator experiencing creation. Expect new and unexpected things to show up in your life.

PART V

The Roles We Play

Now that you have concrete tools to use, let's dive a little deeper into healing and how to incorporate these tools in daily life. The meditation will remind you of who you are and your connection to Oneness. You can do it until the connection becomes as natural as your breath or heartbeat. Gratitude, if practiced regularly, will provide you with a solid direction and set the tone for your daily experiences. Forgiveness is the clearing and tune up work of the past as well as the challenges yet to come.

Diving Deeper Into Forgiveness

When looking at healing through forgiveness of persons or events, there are four roles we play that must be examined. First and most obvious is the victim, who shows up any time

125

you are slighted or wronged. Second the perpetrator, third the observer of wrongdoing, and fourth and last, the member of a group that has or has been victimized. Forgiveness must be extended from each aspect if you want to move on. Otherwise people and events become the chains that hold you in a space of confinement, and this will eventually lead to suffering. It is important to recognize that at one point or another we have all played each role in the game of life.

> *Take a moment to write down the first thing that comes to mind with each point below. Don't spend too much time searching your past, start with whatever is at the top of your head. Other issues will surface in time.*
> *Name one situation where someone did you wrong.*
> *Think of one situation where you did something wrong or hurtful to someone else.*
> *Did you ever observe someone else being mistreated? Name a situation where you stood by and did nothing.*
> *Name an issue that involves a group you belong to, this could be family, race, political affiliation, nationality, gender etc, that has been mistreated and victimized, or that mistreated others.*

In Chapter 10 Leanne and Cameron's stories illustrate the forgiving and healing process from the victim role. They both had things done to them. In this section, I will focus on the other three roles to enable you to let go of the structures that are not always so easy to see, acknowledge and shift.

Chapter 13

Healing And Forgiving Yourself For...

With the exception of a few psychologically challenged people, everyone knows the difference between right and wrong. Deep down we are aware of our own integrity, the place where we are in tune with ourselves, with others and the Oneness of the universe. We are also born with a very strong will to survive and that will can often affect our perception of integrity. Even though we are born knowing what is right and what is wrong, we are easily willing to sacrifice acting on that knowledge if it ensures our survival. But no matter how much our survival depends on our actions, we are accountable for what we do.

This universe is one of cause and effect. All of our actions affect the environment, move molecules and emotions and beget a reaction. It is important to observe yourself and your actions even down to thoughts and words, because they all call forth a reaction. Becoming aware of your actions and deliberately being in charge of them is called "living consciously." I have never met anyone who is capable of always being conscious of his or her actions and thoughts. I am certainly not always consciously aware of my thoughts and even my deeds. But even if it may not be our intent to hurt someone, an impulsive word or action, unconsciously tossed, can sometimes injure another.

As children we learn by trial and error about the feelings and well-being of others around us. Just like dropping a toy and watching it fall to the ground teaches us about gravity, a child also learns that when he or she lashes out and hurts someone, the other person reacts. The reactions vary depending on the other person and can be anger, sadness, pulling away, crying, making light of the situation, or some other display of pain.

When we become aware of the reaction caused in the other person, our survival kicks in. Will the person retaliate? If so, how do we protect ourselves from retaliation? And how can we deal with the shame of knowing that we started it. There is only one way. We talk ourselves into having done the right thing. He had it coming, I needed to defend something, everyone is better of because of it, etc. Instead of stepping into compassion, healing and owning up to my not so right and honorable action, I step into justification. We justify what we've done and disconnect from our integrity.

In the moment it seems easier to excuse our actions as a form of self-defense, rather than apologize and humbly correct our own behavior. From here it can escalate into squabbles, fights and even wars. Many wars have started because people were convinced that they were gravely hurt and deprived of survival needs by "other" people.

Integrity Versus Justification

Integrity is connected to life-force flow so when we operate from integrity we operate within Oneness and the flow is increased. But when integrity is compromised and we hold onto justification, we step out of Oneness. We diminish flow and separate ourselves from ourselves, each other, and the life-force-energy in Oneness. The grids in our structure become like clogged arteries.

If nothing is done to clean the arteries, serious life threatening conditions appear, causing debilitating conditions or death. Of course, this doesn't happen right away, it builds up over time. Justification is similar to a bypass operation. This kind of operation does not address the root of the clogged arteries, but it does restore flow for a limited amount of time. Unless action is taken, such as proper diet, exercise etc., the bypass arteries will eventually clog as well.

Justifying behaviors doesn't change, solve or resolve action but it will alleviate pressure for a brief time. And if we turn to justification time and time again, we will soon rely on this method of moving through things. Our future actions will tend to be congruent with justification instead of integrity, because that is the new bypass artery used for energy flow. Instead of moving through you and your life, the power of flow is rerouted into a trap of justification and focus is put on why we had to step out of integrity instead of living within integrity.

When we do this often enough, we find it difficult to connect to the integrity that was once second nature. We lose track of our inner compass. Many of us notice that other people step in and out of integrity all the time and since those people appear to live well, we think it is ok to do it too.

In the end it doesn't matter if we did what we did because everyone else did it, or because we felt hurt or threatened. What does matter is that we recognize what we did and then forgive ourselves for it. Justification will keep you in the past while self-forgiveness will allow you to move forward, back into integrity and then flow.

We are made up of the stories we tell about ourselves and we all have a few that are built around justifications. Pick one of these stories and let's see if you can get out of justification and back into flow.
"I had to because…"
"It wasn't my fault because…"

There is no room for shame here, we are all perpetrators as well as victims. And remember we are perpetrators even if we have a good excuse for our behavior.

Take the story you have chosen and then look at the harmful action without judgment for a moment. Extract it from the story and simply look at the action. That action probably came about for one of two reasons: either you were acting out of survival, or you were unconscious of the effects of your actions in the moment.

If you were unconscious of the effects of your actions and became aware of them as soon as the other person let you know, you can apologize, repair the damage and let it go without dragging it on. But if you were in a situation where you were hurting someone while fully being aware of your actions, even if these actions were justifiable through self-defense or to ensure your own survival, you need a more involved process to forgive and move on.

For example, if you were in a war and had to kill or harm, you still have to face the fact that you were the perpetrator and the harmed person was the victim. You too may have been the victim of the people who put you in the position, but in this section we are looking at the times you played the perpetrator and how to heal that. You cannot fully heal until you have healed all aspects of the situation.

So now with the action you have chosen, let's return to the four steps explained in Chapter 10 to forgive and heal yourself.

1. *Acknowledge the situation as part of your path, part of who you are at this moment. The situation no matter how it happened was a stepping stone for you to become who you are right now, at the opportunity to expand yourself into increased flow of life-force-energy. Take responsibility for the scene in your life.*
2. *Apologize to the spirit of the person you have harmed and to all the spirits that have been harmed by your action and ask to be forgiven.*
3. *In great gratitude thank everyone involved for having allowed you to learn what you needed to learn and to become the person you are now at this moment.*
4. *Release the scene and everyone involved back into life-force-energy from your heart with love by saying I love you.*

Remember that unless you are capable of literal time-travel, you can never undue your past actions, but you can forgive, heal and move on. If your behavior required serving a punishment, do the punishment knowing that you are repairing your connection to integrity. To help you process your own perpetrator roles I have included the following two stories.

A Simple Story

I bit my sister when I was 3 or 4 years old. She still has a small scar from it. Every time I look at her I am reminded of my action. I tried to reason with myself for years that I was too young to know what I was doing, that I acted in self-defense, that she really asked for it. Sometimes I could even go as far as that it was part of her life experience and therefore I was just helping her experience pain and disfigurement. Well the scar is

131

very small and she is still very beautiful so the damage is not as horrible as it may sound here.

She is three years older than I am and at that time she was much stronger and bigger. She never did anything wrong, a truly good person, who understood what she was told by adults. I looked up to her and wished I could be just like her, but I was not that good of a person. My desires got in the way.

One day, I hoped that if no one noticed I could get away with doing the wrong thing. On that day I really wanted a piece of candy. My parents never had candy or sweets for us and we lived far away from others so naturally I was deprived of the pleasures of sweets. We had a nanny, however, who kept black liquorish, my favorite, in her desk drawer. When she was out in the yard I decided to help myself to a piece of her candy. Nobody would ever notice.

Of course my sister knew I was up to no good and followed me. I was already holding the candy in my hand when she told me to put it back. I didn't want to so she grabbed my hands and held them behind my back to prevent me from sticking it in my mouth. I know she wanted to save me from doing something wrong but I felt trapped, unable to physically defend myself. In desperation I leaned forward and used the only tool left: I bit her.

She forgave me moments later, thought that I was too young to understand etc. but I carried it with me year after year. It always stood between us. I tried to reason with myself, telling myself that I was too young to know impulse control, that stealing candy wasn't that bad, everyone steals sometime, she shouldn't have physically overpowered me, I was just a kid and on and on.

But the bad taste remained until I journeyed through the four steps. I looked at the scene without judgment taking full responsibility for the situation and the learning it provided. I apologized to my sister and myself from my deepest core and asked to be forgiven from the universe. I thanked her with great gratitude for having allowed me to learn an important lesson through her pain. And with a heart felt "I love you", I released the issue, my shame, my guilt and my pain to the universe.

She had long forgiven me and I had served the punishment my parents gave me for the crime, but the issue kept coming up again and again until I forgave myself and moved on. I know this is a small issue and you may think it is not worthy of discussion here, but small or big issues are not very different from one another as the next example will show.

Tom's Story

Tom was drafted into the military when he was eighteen years old. His military training convinced him that there is an enemy out there who is threatening not only his personal survival but the survival of his peers, family, and way of life. At some point he was shipped out to war. The part of his heart and brain that knew killing is wrong was replaced by the need to survive. He did what other soldiers do, killed to survive and aided in the survival of his fellow soldiers.

Years after the war, when I met him, he rarely talked about his experiences. One day he said, "I've killed more people than anyone can love in a lifetime." Even though rationally he had convinced himself that he did what he had to do, he was suffering. He knew that he could not bring any of the people he had killed back to life. No matter how much he justified his actions, they still ate away at his soul and well-being.

I offered Tom a new possibility, to see himself connected to everything and everyone within the energy of the universe. Since everything was part of the same overall energy, it was also part of him. This meant there was a way to forgive and heal this past situation. This is how he started on his journey of healing. He utilized the four steps. He repeated them for every action that needed to be healed and released.

First he acknowledged that even though he was told to kill, he was the one doing the killing. Then he recalled the first time he pulled the trigger. He visualized the person and then the person's infrastructure of family and loved ones. He realized that the person he killed was not the only victim but that pain spread from this person to all the other people connected to him. He saw the tears of the mother, wife and children. Tom is very sensitive and he understood how his action caused not just pain but also triggered the survival instinct in the people connected to the person he had killed. This generated more hatred, more pain and more killing. Tom was overcome with emotion. He humbly apologized in his mind to the person he had killed, who had allowed him to have this revelation in this moment of truth. He asked to be forgiven for his actions by the person and the person's infrastructure for all the pain he had caused. In the moment of realization a whole world opened up for Tom, he saw the connection in all actions around him.

To him it was an awakening, a gift that shifted his perception, his capacity for love increased and his life was flooded with life-force-energy. Grateful for all the understanding, learning and the experience of clarity and love, he implemented step three by thanking everyone involved. Tom understood that this part of his life helped open his eyes to a bigger truth and he forgave himself and with a grateful heart released the issue to the universe with love, as described in step four.

He repeated the four steps to healing for every incident he could think of, where he was the perpetrator. His outlook on life changed, his work situation changed, his relationships became deeper and more love filled. Tom also understood that in the course of our soul experiences we have all done things that are not in harmony with our integrity. While nothing he could do could bring the people back to this life and erase the pain, he could learn to release and move on to live more in harmony with his integrity. He realized that if he had stayed in justification he would be willing to continue to be involved in more wars and other activities that justify behaviors he felt were wrong.

Remember, we are all the space of God moving through structures and experiences and there is nothing that cannot be forgiven. When we forgive ourselves we open up the grids and expand. When we hold a grudge or judge ourselves or others, we tighten the grids and cause pain and suffering and our soul can't expand. When you judge yourself, you become judgmental toward others, constantly trying to correct your own mistakes in others.

When you justify, you seek situations that call for the same kind of justification. In other words you need to have other people around you that also compromise their integrity so that you can continue to justify your behavior. If someone has forgiven him- or herself, he or she is now capable of looking at someone else, who is doing the same thing, with compassion and love instead of judgment. Therefore instead of condemning them they can offer help and maybe prevent the other person from making the same mistake. That is called being the change you want to see.

Chapter 14

Healing The Observer

Every day we get to observe our actions and their effects but we also get to observe the people and events around us. What we notice on a daily basis are wonderful opportunities to keep us moving through life consciously. Once we are open to the Oneness of the universe – us being a part of everything and everything being a part of us - whatever we encounter in essence becomes our responsibility. And we can transform it, with a smile, a kind word or by setting an example of doing things differently. But first we need to clean our own side of the street. If there are unresolved issues within ourselves, and there always are, we need to tend to them first so we can be free of judgment when we approach others.

In the last chapter we worked on healing the perpetrator self, how to forgive ourselves for things we have done directly to others while not being in sync with our integrity. Here we will look at our role as the observer, the *innocent* bystander. Let's break this role into two specific types. One is the present bystander who directly witnesses the transgression, like standing next to someone getting their pockets picked. Two is the remote bystander who hears or reads about an event like a bombing overseas or a case of child abuse in the same city.

In order to get a feel for the two kinds of bystander roles, take a moment and write down some things that you heard of, read about or encountered in the last 24 hours that you considered not right. Separate your issues into two categories:
With my own eyes I witnessed:
I did not get involved because....
I read/ heard about:
I did not get involved because...

Both types of innocent bystander are focused on survival rather than on integrity. Maybe a more fitting name for innocent bystander is fearful bystander. Because innocence leaves the moment we become aware of something taking place that we consider not congruent with our integrity. Immediately our mind kicks in with questions about our own survival and how it would affect us if we got involved. The inner protector says close your eyes, look the other way or why isn't anybody else doing anything about it. We distance ourselves from the event to insure our unharmed survival.

Present Bystander

Let's address the present bystander. Look at your past and see if there are any events where you stood by and watched something you thought was wrong without interfering. This could be anything from watching a serious crime, a kid being bullied in school, an abusive argument, or anything that you notice as being wrong.

Write down one situation where you were the observer.

As we move through the next examples follow along with your situation. The observer is a very loaded role. When you are the victim, you can deny any wrong doing on your part, because the bad thing happened to you. When you are the perpetrator you know what you did and why and you can justify it with a good story.

The Observer has two issues to deal with. First, by allowing something to happen to someone else you are like the perpetrator, actively involved. Second, you are somewhat of a victim, a victim of your decision to not get involved. Surely like all the other roles we have good explanations for our behavior. These range from survival, fear of what is going to happen to us if we get involved, to this is none of our business. Or we can even go as far as to say it is that person's experience, and I am going to allow him or her to have it. But it is our business, everything in our universe is our business and deep down inside, in our place of integrity, we know it is.

If you have problems finding an issue in your life, I usually suggest thinking about high school. During those years, when everyone is trying to figure out how to fit in, structures and shields are built to protect and hide in. If nobody knows who I really am, I am safe, because they can't touch me, or my deepest feelings. Boys are taught not to cry and if they do, they need to be sure to do it in secret. Being open and connected is replaced by a dense strong structure of individual survival. Following is a story to illustrate the present bystander.

139

A High School Story

When I was 11 years old I went to boarding school. Far away from the protection of my own home and room so I had to install a protective structure immediately. Like all the other new kids, I was tested for emotional strength. I was odd and didn't really fit in. I also had the ability to recede into the background and become almost invisible. I kept my fears and feelings locked away inside and pretended to be strong and untouched by everything around me. It worked, I was not really there and engaged only on the surface with others.

After I was well established and knew how to maneuver within my protective grid, a new girl came to the school and to our room. At that time we were six in a room. She was different and the popular group of girls did not like her. I had met her before she came to the school and tried to show her around and be a friend. But being her friend meant that I was opening my protective structure to the abuse of the girls in charge. So I kept my interactions to a minimum and was nice to everyone equally.

One night, a group of girls came into our room. Everyone was sleeping or so it seemed. They taunted and tortured the new girl, she cried and I could feel her fear from across the room. I lay there frozen in my bed, my mind told me to pretend to be deeply asleep and so I did. Nobody ever talked about that night. The new girl was quiet because I am sure she didn't want to subject herself to more, I was quiet because I didn't want to be next and life went on. The new girl eventually left the school and for a while we remained friends, but I couldn't be real friends with her. I had been a coward and not a friend.

As the years went by, she stayed on my mind. Even though during subsequent hazing of other people. I would speak out to make up for that night, it never really did. Much later, when I was in therapy, my therapist told me that I was just a kid and I should not be so hard on myself. But it didn't help. Finally I

140

contacted the girl and apologized. She had moved on and hadn't even thought about me in association with the event. She thought it was nuts that I was still thinking about it.

One day I learned the four steps to forgiving and letting go and I sat in my favorite chair. In my mind I recalled the whole scene. I realized that the scene and the victim as well as the perpetrators had come together in my play of life to help me understand life and the universe on a deeper level. The perpetrators had sacrificed their integrity to help me understand mine. The victim had endured her pain so I could learn and see. I apologized to everyone in the scene and said in my mind and heart: *I am sorry, please forgive me. I am so grateful to all you did for me and I thank you.* As I spoke the final words *I love you*, I allowed the scene to dissolve into the universe.

Years later when I went for a reunion I was able to enjoy myself. I could sit next to the women involved and feel nothing but gratitude. It was amazing.

This was a fairly easy example and didn't really threaten the life of anyone involved. But what about if you observed a big crime and remained silent? It is not different from a little crime. If you remain in guilt, you will remain in your dense structure of self-protection and in addition to stifling your life-force you will also allow poisonous guilt to run through your structure eating away at your life. In the end, this does not help anyone else and it will destroy you. Heal and forgive the situation and expand yourself so that next time you will act differently not as a guilty form of self-punishment but to experience increased life-force as it moves through you and the others involved.

It is incredibly important that you do not come from judgment in any way, when you observe situations. Always remember that you are Oneness, that the same energy that moves through the situation also moves through you. Judgment is separation and love is unison. If you go back far enough in any situation you will find out why it is happening the way it is. There are always constructs that prevent the flow of life-force-energy within people that cause them to act in a way that is not congruent with integrity and love. Instead of judging yourself and others, focus on opening up the structures and allow more flow into the situation into yourself and everyone involved.

As you go through your day become conscious of what is in your life.

If you are witnessing something, which is not in unison with your integrity you are affected by it, sometimes even more than if you were the perpetrator. Everything in this universe is part of you and you hold a responsibility for it.

Remote Bystander

Addressing events from the remote bystander perspective is a little more tricky, because often there is little you can do to effect the situation directly in the moment. But those events also offer opportunities for us to grow and continually align ourselves with our own integrity and set a path for others to follow.

If you watch the news, read the newspaper or are otherwise engaged in what is happening in the world, you are constantly confronted with issues that go against your innate integrity. There is killing, torture, people starving etc. In order to survive you think you have to desensitize yourself and justify. You could distance yourself by believing that it is their path, believing that they choose this in order to achieve their learning. That is not wrong, we all have our experiences and situations arise so that we learn and evolve, but the focus here is not on other people, it is on you, observing as a voyeur a situation, which goes against your integrity.

The fact that you experience feelings while you become aware of a situation indicates that it is your business. You are involved not only with your mind, as you read about it but also with your body as you can probably feel it. The story affects you because there is something that needs healing within you. Here is a little tool I like to use to help me stay conscious and act from the best part of me.

> *When you witness a situation, don't just look the other way or fold the newspaper and throw it away, or click to a new webpage. Instead ask yourself the following:*
> *How do I feel about this?*
> *How does this event or story relate to my life?*
> *Which personal incidences does this story remind me off, that I haven't healed yet?*
> *What is going to happen to my survival if I stand up for my integrity?*
> *Which step can I take right now in my life to be more in sync with my integrity?*

For example if you read about a hate crime, search for hate within yourself, if you read about a stress induced crime, search for stress induced anger within yourself and so on. When going through the four steps make sure you acknowledge that the person you read about did this so you can heal yourself and become aware of your own hate and anger, then continue the steps as if it were a personal event. Following is an example to illustrate healing the self through the remote bystander role.

An Animal Story

A few years ago a politician made headlines with her love for hunting. For many people it was an outrage that anyone loves to hunt just for sport and not for food. It bothered me too, and every time I went to the supermarket and passed the meat isle I thought about her. Years ago I used to eat meat but

I didn't hunt for it, I bought it already dead on the shelf neatly packed and unrecognizable.

When the stories of her hunting made headlines I was reminded of my meat eating past and all the animals that had to suffer for me. I continued with the self-forgiving and four steps to heal and let go. I understood that seeing meat in the supermarket did not get me to really think about myself, but someone as over the top as this politician got my attention, so I followed through the steps with her as the helpful spirit.

Now I am not judgmental anymore about other people eating meat. It may not be an issue for someone else. Also, I know I was just like that at some point and I understand. Instead of getting angry and judgmental I can talk about this issue without trying to change anyone. I can share my story and talk about my feeling on hunting and meat and that for me eating meat is like carrying the pain of the animals in my body, something I choose not to do. This belief alone will stimulate a thought process and maybe change for some people.

Chapter 15

Healing The World
Structures That Involve Groups Of People

We all belong to a group or tribe. We are born in countries, reside in places and are affected by the beliefs and politics of the groups we belong to either by choice, location or birth. These groups influence who we are and become part of our existing structures.

For example I was born in Germany. Even though I was fortunate to have been born into a family that was part of the underground movement during the NAZI regime, I still have to deal with Germany's past and the way people view it. Of course I can always pretend to be from another nearby country to avoid any discussion or emotions directed at Germans. But if I were say African American, the color of my skin would not allow for that kind of out. Race and nationality are large groups we belong to, but there are smaller groups and tribes we belong to as well, like groups that share our sexual orientation, political views, gender, religions, spiritual beliefs, gangs etc.

When we are part of a group we are part of the structure of the group. These structures claim to support us and keep us safe. It is the *one for all* mentality, the group has got your back and you are safe.

Group constructs function the same as individual constructs. Groups have ideas about their identity and the way things should operate around them. Since some form of belief is behind the group construct, it is usually very rigid. Group structure implies that its members are right, no matter which side they are on. Often if those beliefs are challenged, the survival fear gets triggered. As a matter of fact, in order to form a strong group and define its boundaries an outside enemy can be very useful.

As soon as an outside influence threatens the ideals or individuals of a group, the group becomes stronger. This is why leaders of a tribe will often tell its members that their survival is threatened by an individual or another group in order to gain power. If a peaceful resolution is not achieved, conflict soon follows, leading to war and horrible crimes, like genocide or enslavement. Some of these events may seem unforgivable, and I agree that it may not be easy to forgive such crimes. But not forgiving keeps you within the construct that created the crimes in the first place and will ultimately create more of the same.

Take a look at history and you will see that these events repeat time and time again.
What groups do you belong to?
Has your group done things in the past that are not congruent with your integrity?
Did you or the groups you belong to experience victimization by another group?

146

What are some of the issues and events that you find "unforgivable"?

Forgiving may be difficult at times but if your desire to move on is strong enough, you will find your way through the difficulty. It is simply a letting go of old baggage, a stepping out of the structure that created the pain and expanding into new possibilities. The groups or leaders whom you need to forgive are not really involved in the process.

Many times, the people we hold responsible for our pain are no longer around. Let's take Hitler for example. Holding onto the pain he created in the lives of so many people does not affect him, but it does affect the persons that hold onto that pain. Forgiving doesn't mean going into denial about events or even forgetting that the event ever happened. Forgiving is taking the pain from history out of the present moment. We will return to the tool for releasing this kind of pain, but first let's take a look at why this kind of group healing has to be done on an individual level.

Events that affect large groups of people are highly energized by the many people and interacting structures and webs that feed into them. This creates the illusion that healing can occur on a group level, but it can't. All healing takes place individually. No person can actually heal or change another but that person can heal him or herself and then guide large groups of people towards a space for self-healing. Mahatma Gandhi phrased it well when he said: "be the change you want to see in the world". Dr. Martin Luther King Jr. led people into his vision by moving in the direction himself. You are responsible for yourself and by healing yourself you can create a path for others to walk. As I said before, healing does not mean going into denial or forgetting history.

Let's liken it to a person with a terminal illness. Due to a new medical discovery, life style adjustment or a miracle, this person recovers from the previously terminal illness. Immediately the term terminal doesn't apply anymore and the possibility for a cure is a reality for everyone facing the same terminal illness. The healed person is not going to walk around stating that she or he was never sick. That would be denying that it ever happened and with that the awareness and possibility of curing it for the future would also vanish.

The change comes from a full awareness of what happened and then overcoming it and creating a path for healing. There is no promise that everyone will be cured or that our example person will never get sick again, but it does show that healing is possible one person at a time. And when healing occurs in any one person it advances the healing process for anyone in our Universe. Because we are all connected, by healing yourself of an issue you open the door to healing for anyone with similar issues. You forge a path, like an explorer and become a model of possible change.

Think about an example in your life, a personal experience or a historic one where one person led the way to change.
Write down at least one time when you befriended someone from a different group and discovered that they were in fact not so different from yourself. If nothing comes to mind, think of high school.

When my kids were toddlers I joined playgroups so that they could make friends. The common factor among the parents of the group was that we all had kids the same age. For the most part this was the only common denominator and, without that playgroup, I don't think our paths would have ever crossed. We walked and lived in different worlds. But we all had the one common desire for our kids to be healthy, happy and safe. For the kids sake we spent hours together and despite differing lifestyles, economic backgrounds, political opinions or religions, each of us became more tolerant of one another.

The big lesson most of us learned was to look for the similarities rather than the differences. Find the points that bring us together rather than focus on the judgment that separates us. If this kind of tolerance were universal, the world would be a much more peaceful place. Remember, we all have a common denominator, even if the only one we can find is being human.

Judgment Divides And Love Unites

As we've explored in the previous chapters, structures cause separation especially when judgments are involved. The moment you believe that you are your structure or you adhere too closely to it, you are in judgment of others. When you judge someone else, you are also judging yourself to be different.

Judgment is based on duality, a right always has a wrong. Imagine judgment is a cancer. It is the one cell in the organism of the universe that decides to be better or different from the rest. It sets itself apart and starts growing according to its own agenda, creating tumors and eventually poisoning the system. This works on all sides of an issue and on all bodies the same.

For example if you are a minority being judged by others and you yourself start to judge, you are doing the same thing. You are becoming just like the people you dislike. It is a vicious cycle and can only be broken if you step out of it. If you remain within, the duality will increase in strength and the issues will resurface in horrible proportions over and over again.

The only way to step out of it is to step into Oneness and to discover that we are essentially all the same energy flow. Love your enemies, your neighbors and everyone you meet. But loving anyone first requires us to truly love ourselves, because in doing that we are no longer affected and subject to judgment. Anger, hate, insecurity and fear are all vehicles that feed on opposition and negativity. Once we remove the target for the arrows of judgment, we stop producing fuel and those

149

vehicles soon run out of gas. Of course while they are still fueled they can create a lot of devastation and pain, but if we hold steadfast and are patient the gas will run out.

I am not saying this is easy, I am saying it is worth it, even if it takes a lot of courage to be yourself. Find the common denominator, the basic love that unites. This may have to be something like breathing air, loving your children, enjoying good food, etc. and use the basis of that as the love that unites. What may keep us from being the explorer is the fear of standing alone or even of being killed for it, like many have been. But the fact is we all will leave this human structure and transition through death. The question becomes do we want to live life limited, in fear and misery, allowing a limited flow of universal love energy to flow through, or are we willing to step into expansion and look toward an increased flow of love within and without?

So how do we heal group related issues? The same way we heal personal ones. You have to realize that only you can heal the world, end the wars, end racism and all other group related ailments, and it is easy. If you find yourself judging anything or anybody, you are responding from the internal pain of self-judgment, and all you have to do is heal that.

The moment you have a judgmental thought stop yourself and ask:
What pain within myself is asking to be healed?

Imagine you carry a painful fire pit inside yourself, which is burning up your resources for well-being. Every time you have a judgmental thought or, even more powerful, a judgmental reaction you throw wood and fuel into your fire, and every time you stop yourself and proceed to heal the issue, you extinguish part of the flame until one day it is no longer there.

When I am paying attention to my thoughts I find that many of them are judgmental. All I have to do is open a newspaper, walk into a grocery store, or even hang out with friends.

I am constantly confronted with issues that are attached to one of my belief systems. But I try to stop my thoughts as they arise because the truth is, there is nothing I have come across, which on some level, I haven't thought about doing myself. I did not act on most of those things but I have had thoughts about them.

Let's take Hitler and the NAZI regime. There were many times growing up that I wished they never existed, times I wanted revenge for the feelings they caused. I even thought that people like them don't deserve to walk the earth, should be killed, etc. Let's stop right there. How are my thoughts different from what happened during the Hitler reign? I am ashamed to say that the thoughts I had toward the perpetrators of the Holocaust were not that different from the actions they performed during that time.

Whenever I realize that my consciousness is occupied with repetitive duality I stop myself. I instantly know not to throw the first stone and condemn something I myself am guilty of in some regard. Instead of condemning and judging I look at it as a call to healing. I look at it as a step to create heaven on earth, and it all has to start with me. This is where I use the 4 step process again, so I can see how the very people I condemn are here to raise my awareness about my own healing process and my consciousness. Racism, nationalism and religious beliefs are core issues with many people. These structures involve multitudes and can only shift one at a time until the tipping point is reached and the whole construct shifts.

As you process this chapter, I suggest you start with a small issue like the example of the playgroup and then move on to bigger issues. Take the little issues of daily life, and just keep in mind if there is judgment inside of you, there is also something to heal. For those little issues I play the 4 step process like a game.

Here's one to illustrate my point. I live in Los Angeles and have many judgments about other drivers. Even though none of them has done anything that I am not guilty of. The other day, I was in a rush, my daughter was in the passenger seat and we were behind the slowest driver in recent memory. I got very upset and many unkind thoughts ran through my mind and escaped my lips. After a bit, my daughter turned to me and said "people only get upset about stuff they do themselves, just like me, I do it all the time." And she was right. I immediately became aware of my behavior and realized the problem was with me. I had left late, I stepped out of my integrity by not allowing others to be themselves, I replaced my compassion with haste and anger, which I directed at another being. I instantly apologize to the Universe and I ask the energy running through the other driver to please forgive me. In gratitude for all the help I received in becoming more aware and conscious, I thank him and released him with love.

In short I just say: I apologize, please forgive me, I thank you and I love you. I am now a much more relaxed driver, and when I'm not I have a tool to help.

This example was easy enough but what if I want to heal and transform something as big as racism, the steps are the same, but the attached emotions run deeper. It requires us to move deeper into the issue and the emotion.

For example an African American person who is confronted by a white person calling him derogatory names or even threatening his life, would have to stop and look within, at all the emotions that come up, and see this event as an opportunity to shift and heal the entire grid, instead of reacting with anger and dislike. This means that he or she has to step out of duality and recognize Oneness life-force energy in the opponent, he or she has to step out of judgment and into unity. She or he has to recognize this event as a call to healing his or her own judgment and maybe even hatred.

When you see yourself as equal beings or structures in the Universe that contain the same life force energy, hatred and judgments vanish and expansion will happen. But how do you best achieve this with a big deeply engrained personal issue that involves your entire race? First you have to separate yourself from the group energy, an energy that has also served as protection in your life, and is therefore closely attached to you. The group has served as a means of survival and stepping away from it is exposing vulnerability.

Once you can see yourself as an individual being you can start looking at the issues of judgment and even hate as your personal growth opportunity by healing them on an individual basis. After you have achieved the personal healing you have not only expanded your own Life-force-energy flow but you are also the one leading the way toward a peaceful new world.

Like I said, healing a group or the whole universe can only be done one person at the time so don't put it off, pay attention to your judgments. Use the 4 steps, they work incredibly fast and efficiently, after a while you will recognize your limiting and judging thoughts as calls to heal and expand yourself and through you the whole world.

Here are some questions to ask yourself and ponder:
Since all groups request that I give up part of my individuality in return for my membership, what did I give up?
Did I give up any of my integrity?
How many issues can I heal today?
How many thoughts did I have today or words did I speak today that encouraged duality and fueled a problem rather than helped heal it?

If we could always be in a state of forgiveness we would not have to recreate the same history over and over. Like attracts like is one of the laws of nature. Hate and pain will only attract and create more hate and pain. But forgiveness and love will attract more forgiveness and love and create a better life for everyone.

PART VI

Endless Possibilities

When we understand the structure that defines us and the flow that is us, the possibilities are endless.

Chapter 16

Mastering Structure And Flow

Now that you have gotten to this point in the book, you have a clear understanding of how structure works in your life. Whether you are in the process of cleaning out past baggage or just considering it, my hope for you is that you continue to move towards Oneness. This means constantly letting go of separation and judgment. And as we learned in the previous chapters, the focus is not on the separation and judgment you want to release, but on the love you want to become.

If you are in a situation calling for reaction imagine that you are pure love energy and before you react ask yourself:
How would love react?
Here is another questions you can ask yourself to attune to the Oneness and love that you are.
What would love do?

Be open to letting go of the ideas you had about how to react and do what love would do. When you start to do this you will soon see your life expanding in beautiful ways. Of course the universe has a way of testing your new skill and challenges may come up causing you to slip into unconscious reactions without even noticing until the situation has passed. But being aware of your reaction and looking at it without judgment will help cultivate the expansion that Oneness brings.

Following is a little example from my life to illustrate how easy it is to slip into unconscious reaction and how easy it can be to get back on track.

A few years ago I was meditating on questions about holding the space of love. I was in the middle of reading Glenda Green's amazing book *The Keys of Jeshua*. At that moment my life felt perfect. I was interrupted by the doorbell and got up feeling all-powerful and good, expecting some form of miracle or long lost friend to be at the door. Instead what I found was a man proselytizing and accusing me of being evil. As he spoke, he managed to wedge his foot in the open door so that I was unable to close it. Needless to say, I got very angry, said unkind things and even threatened to hurt the man's foot if he did not remove it from my door.

Eventually he did and as I walked back to my meditation chair, I stopped in my tracks remembering that I had just affirmed to myself that I could hold the space of love even in situations of adversity. I was humbled and realized that although I had come from unconscious reaction, I was able to recognize it within moments. I immediately set my intent to hold the space of love again and do better next time. I definitely had room to improve and that was the direction I intended to go. Although on some level I failed the easy test, I was grateful for the opportunity to learn from it. The amazing thing was that I found out later that the man did not ring any of my neighbor's doorbells.

Acknowledge your structure and move toward expanded flow.
Set the intent for your direction and move toward it, if it were
all smooth you wouldn't know that you achieved anything.

Once you have created evidence of flow and expansion the possibilities are endless. We are all the same life-force energy, entering and flowing into and through different structures and grids all the time. Therefore if we really wanted to and if we were truly free from any attachment to our structures, we could shift and move around into any grid or construct we choose. We already do this to some extent when we feel empathy for others. But we do it with a small part of our consciousness and remain attached to our own structures, especially the physical one. But what if we could let go of all attachment? What could happen then and is it even possible?

This is a phenomenon that has been described in different ways and degrees of possibilities. For example if a person shifts into the awareness of another person, an animal or power totem to retrieve special insight it's called shape shifting. Shape shifting is practiced by Native Americans and other cultures. Or channeling, a practice of allowing another being to use one's body structure to communicate. Neither shape shifting nor channeling require being highly evolved and there are plenty of stories and witness accounts of them happening all around the world.

There are, of course, those beings that are highly evolved who have mastered detachment from structure and are said to have appeared in the form of a burning bush, a homeless person, an enlightened being, an animal or a vision of some sort. But even these highly evolved beings are the same life-force-energy as you and I.

You probably heard the phrase: "It is easier for a camel to pass through the eye of a needle, than for a rich man to enter into the kingdom of heaven." This is about attachment and the more attachment you carry the harder it is to enter into the great Oneness.

Be aware of your structures, the physical, mental emotional and spiritual ones, examine them and remember, whatever belief system you are embedded in has the strongest hold on you. Whether it is a religion or science or the absence of a religion doesn't matter. An alien world as well as our world is a constructed grid. Even time is a construct, a structure of the mind and doesn't really exist; therefore if mastered, shifting can happen between time, space, worlds and dimension.

I'd like to leave you with the biggest and easiest way to move toward Oneness:
Be the best you that you can be at any time.
Realize that everything and everyone is connected and a part of you, so whether you hurt or love someone, you are doing it to yourself.
Be the love–life–force–energy that you are.
Enjoy your expansion.

Continuous expansion is eternal life.

81409624R00091

Made in the USA
San Bernardino, CA
08 July 2018